THE FIRST-TIME
SALES MANAGER

THE FIRST-TIME
SALES MANAGER

Jeremy G. Thorn

MERCURY

First published in May 1990
by Mercury Books
Reprinted September 1991
by Mercury Books
Gold Arrow Publications Ltd
862 Garratt Lane
London SW17 0NB

Set in Plantin by Phoenix Photosetting
Printed and bound in Great Britain by
Mackays of Chatham PLC, Chatham, Kent

Cartoons by Keith Reynolds

British Library Cataloguing in Publication Data

Thorn, Jeremy G.
The first-time sales manager.
1. Sales management
I. Title
658.8′1

ISBN 1–85252–050–7

Contents

v

CONTENTS

Useful Exercises

Acknowledgements

My thanks go to all those who have helped to put these thoughts together. I would like to make special mention of all those friends and colleagues, past and present, who have given me their unstinted support and enthusiasm, and shared a passion for excellence. It is they who have made the posts I have enjoyed such a rewarding source of pleasure. I am also most grateful to all my tutors who have given their time and expertise, and the authors of the many excellent books that I have enjoyed reading, some of which are listed at the back. I only regret that all these people are far too numerous to name individually. Without their help there would have been no book.

I am also appreciative of the visual aids provided by Keith Reynolds, whose cartoons always serve to illuminate as well as amuse.

Finally, my very special thanks go to my wife Éilis, and my family, whose support and forbearance have been beyond measure.

Foreword

by Hugh Sharp

Head of Business Development in the Training Agency of the
Department of Employment

After several years of fast growth British companies are facing
greater competitive pressures than ever before. Many of our leading companies are now getting ahead of the pack by making
training a central part of their business strategy. Training on its
own is a cost, not an investment. But training linked to the
achievement of business objectives is a real competitive weapon.

Jeremy Thorn's comprehensive portrait of today's effective
sales manager makes this point admirably. He stresses the importance of treating training as an ongoing investment – not as something available only to new employees. He also highlights the
responsibility of the manager in continuing to develop his or her
staff. Companies which adopt this approach will rapidly see
results in their performance and profits.

February 1990

Preface

'Fanaticism consists of redoubling your efforts when you have forgotten your aim.'
George Santayana

As a new sales representative, I received all the training I could have asked for. I knew my products and my company thoroughly, I was formally trained in the skills and delights of selling and I received frequent visits from my sales manager, who offered me positive and encouraging support. I worked hard at understanding my target markets and how they made purchasing decisions, and I made a point of learning quickly how my competitors operated, their strengths and their weaknesses. I enjoyed being a salesman more than I ever thought I would. Naturally, I made mistakes, but I also enjoyed the successes. Before long, I was keen to acquire greater responsibilities.

Then one day I was told that I was to be appointed an Area Sales Manager. I was delighted. After a while, however, I began to wonder what had changed. I now had someone else to manage, which was interesting and challenging, but somehow I did not feel my job had really altered. After all, I still had my own calls to make and sales targets to meet. No one told me what else was expected of me in my new role.

I decided that I dare not ask my immediate boss exactly what my new duties might be, because I thought (quite rightly, you might feel!) that he might then lose confidence in me. I therefore asked a few of my other colleagues. That took some courage, but they didn't seem to be too sure either. Of course, we all *thought* we knew what we should be doing, but nobody offered any positive reinforcement or guidance.

Years later, I found from meeting other sales managers that their experiences were rarely all that different from mine. On my own initiative, I therefore made a point of attending as many relevant training courses as I could. I also read widely and discussed the management problems that I came across with anyone who would listen. I would like to acknowledge here the help and encouragement all these sources gave me, unreservedly.

But it was so unnecessarily late. It annoyed me that I had been given a new position without a proper description of what was expected from me, or without any thought having been given to the training that the post should have demanded. It annoyed me even more that many others had obviously faced the same experience.

This, then, is the book I would have liked to have had to help me in those early, formative times. It is written to help others through the first stages of acquiring the important and practical skills which distinguish excellent sales managers from the rest. Accordingly, I hope it will also help those already in sales management positions to take a broader view of their role, and allow them to develop their careers further.

Throughout this book, I refer to 'products' in their broadest sense (including all forms of services), whether they are destined for consumer or industrial markets, large or small. Wherever I have used the term salesman, be sure that I include in this generic term saleswomen.

I take for granted that you know how to sell, and indeed what sales people sometimes get up to: I assume you have been in their position too! I have concentrated therefore on other important questions, such as strategic planning and detailed organisation matters – subjects which are intensely practical and not to be learned by making them up as you go along, on a best-efforts basis and as time permits. We no longer live in the age of the enthusiastic amateur, but the hardened professional.

This book is not just for your immediate interest, but for future reference too, by you and those who follow. It is a popular fallacy that sales teams and their managers are too busy to read management and business books. Do, please, prove this wrong! If it were true, I would wish to recall that rather frightening definition of fanaticism: the redoubling of efforts when all sense of direction has been lost. I hope that rather, after reading this book, you will certainly feel refreshed and encouraged to renew your efforts, but will also have a clearer and more certain sense of direction.

JEREMY G. THORN
Sheffield, England
February 1990

Note to this reprint

Since the first edition of this book appeared, kind readers have suggested that the title is unfairly misleading. They have flatteringly suggested that it implies that this book will *only* interest first-time sales managers, when in fact it is arguably of even *greater* value to experienced managers, who will more readily appreciate the importance and relevance of the advice and suggestions it offers.

As it happens, I feel I should blushingly accept the criticism, but as I think that it is still a good title, that my prime intention when writing it was – and still is – to help newcomers to sales management first and foremost, and that I can't think of a better title, it remains with its old one!

Nevertheless, it appears to me indisputable that both employers and employees should, in their own respective enlightened self-interests, take a responsibility for career development and skill enhancement. Accordingly, I hope that this book will truly help both those who are managed and those who manage, both those who are new to sales management and those who are more experienced.

JEREMY G THORN
Sheffield, England
September 1991

I

INTRODUCTION

'Some see private enterprise as a predatory target to be shot at, others as a cow to be milked, but few are those who see it as a sturdy horse pulling the wagon.'

Winston S. Churchill

1 Managing – Not Selling

Managing a sales team requires quite different skills from selling. Of course, as a sales manager, you do have to be able to sell. For example, you will almost certainly wish to retain the responsibility of negotiating the really big deals; you may also have the sales responsibility for key accounts. And why not? Even the best sales skills become rusty without regular practice. You cannot expect to lead and motivate others if you are not able to show your team how to do better.

However, selling skills are not the only ones required of a sales manager. Accordingly, most enlightened companies recognise that the special abilities and personalities, which make for the really super salesman or woman, do not always make for the best sales manager. The sales stars may therefore be better employed by doing what they do best, selling rather than managing. Their managers' task is to ensure that the special sales skills which they bring to any team are fully utilised, challenged and rewarded.

Before we look at the duties of a sales manager in detail, it is worth considering further some of the differences between selling and managing. After all, why *should* the best sales people necessarily make good managers? Look at the conflict of interests and duties highlighted in Figure 1.

Vision

Good sales people need to be empathetic to their customers' needs, but they also need a powerful sense of ego-drive to cross over their

3

Figure 1: Selling – and Managing

THE SALES MAN/WOMAN	THE SALES MANAGER
Personal drive (ego)	Submission of personal needs to the goals of the company (i.e. corporate drive)
Needs to win battles (each visit)	Needs to win the 'war' (i.e. meet those corporate goals)
Able to work alone	Able to work with others
Gets customers to see his point	Gets sales team to see company's point
Sales skills and product knowledge	Management skills and market knowledge
Able to work away from the office	Able to work at the office
Works well with people	Works well with people, figures, paperwork and the hierarchy
Good at sales tactics	Good at sales tactics *and* marketing strategy

customers' doorsteps in order to present themselves, their company and their products. As such, a sales team can be a very difficult collection of individuals to manage.

Your job must be to redirect that individualistic, idiosyncratic ego-drive towards the corporate goals, which you must help identify. This means that you must see what Americans graphically describe as the 'big picture', and thus be able to prioritise key objectives and prevent these being eclipsed by individuals' own personal interpretations of what *they* think they should be doing. To succeed, you need to be just as responsive to your company's goals as you will need to be to your team's individual needs – or your own.

The overall sense of perspective that this demands means that a

4

sales manager must be able to rise above the heat of any particular battle, in order to plan an overall strategy. Your sales team may not always see the big picture, but you must.

Taking the broad and longer-term point of view is something that new sales managers may find particularly difficult. This will especially be the case if the customer or product is one which, as a sales representative, the sales manager has had special experience of and perhaps affection for. With this in mind, here is a timely warning. More than one company in the past has found that precious sales resources have been spent on cultivating traditional customers and territories, markets or products, to the exclusion of other more important – but new – opportunities. Often, this has been due to the mistaken loyalties of a sales manager, unable to see that times have changed. Not many of these companies last to tell the tale, however; nor do their sales teams.

Independence

The best sales managers know that it is vital to balance their time successfully between the team in the field and their colleagues back at base. The balance is also probably changing, however subtly, all the time.

This too can be very difficult for the newly promoted manager. Uneasy with office life and administrative systems, it is a tempting prospect for a new sales manager to spend a disproportionate amount of time in the field. If your style is *always* to lead from the front, you need to be aware that you are probably not really managing. Of course, it is just as damaging *never* to venture out into the market-place; after all, you need to be able to give practical leadership to the sales team and review market forces at first hand. However, having enjoyed the freedom of a roving sales representative, it is very difficult to submit yourself to the confines and disciplines of head office. Nevertheless, it is important to do so.

Many newly promoted managers claim that reconciling the

5

'The best sales managers know that it is vital to balance their time between the team in the field and colleagues back at base.'

Useful Exercise: Days in versus days out

One way to solve the dilemma of how to split your time between the office and your field sales team is to set yourself a target for each month. Some weeks you might have to spend every day in the office, and on other occasions you might find your route takes you out every day, but over a month you can realistically expect to set yourself an overall target of days in the office and days to be spent outside. What that target is will depend on the detail of your job, the particular problems that arise and even the buying-cycle (if there is one). But if you have not met your target at the end of the month, you will need to ask whether it was your target that was adrift, or your planning. Remember, good managers *make* things happen!

---

need to take the broad view, from *within* the office hierarchy and all its politics, is one of the toughest challenges they have to meet.

Scope

The most obvious task that will challenge any newly promoted sales manager is not only that they must manage themselves, they must now also manage others. This requires new skills. Whether these skills are applied with wisdom, fairness and firmness, or otherwise, is another aspect that distinguishes the excellent sales manager from the rest. Distancing oneself from old colleagues and still retaining their respect is not easy, but the better sales managers know that it is essential.

In common with any other newly promoted manager, you will find that making yourself available to your team at any time is part of the job, but being their friend is not. If you go to the pub for lunch, that is your choice. If you stay there late, passing time with some of the team, can you complain if they then stay late when you are *not* there? Being accessible is important, but so is the setting of standards.

Conclusion

Successful sales managers clearly need to know their products, their markets and the major customers well. If they do not, at least they need to be able to learn about them quickly. Further, in order to provide the leadership necessary, it is important to know how to sell, handle objections, present winning proposals, and be fully aware of all the other sales-oriented skills which any sales person needs. But a sales manager does *not* need to be the best salesman or woman on the team, and indeed will probably not be so. Rather, other skills and qualities are required.

These include:

- objectivity and vision,
- planning skills and discipline,
- numeracy,
- an ability to lead, inspire and direct, and
- interpersonal skills.

We shall look at all these issues throughout this book.

2 Dealing with Bosses, Peers and Staff

Many field-sales people find it difficult to relate to colleagues back at head office. Because they spend the bulk of their time with prospects and customers (or at least, should do), it is not surprising that many may appear to identify more closely with their customers than with their own company. This need not necessarily be a bad thing, especially if the company needs to respond better to market demand or competitor pressures. However, this apparently mistaken sense of loyalty can be misinterpreted back at base. As sales manager, you need to be able to translate this accurately for other colleagues, in a way that will not be misunderstood.

- The building of bridges between the sales team and all other functions is therefore a vital role for any sales manager.

This is especially important because many colleagues will have quite different and conflicting tactical goals, even within the same business. Think, for example, of the finance manager who may well be more concerned about protecting today's margins, rather than building tomorrow's markets. Consider the problem of the production manager who knows that he has to reduce scrap rates and improve productivity, but accordingly prefers to concentrate on making the well-known products rather than the new ones.

All managers will have their own goals to meet, each of which may make excellent sense in isolation, but may be quite incompatible when looked at from the broader viewpoint. Only if you too can adequately communicate your needs, can a global consensus be arrived at in line with the overall business objectives to which you all subscribe.

- Accordingly, tact, diplomacy and sensitivity to others' points of view, combined with the ability to persuade colleagues that a contrary view is better when it is appropriate, are crucial for long-term success.

Too many companies fail to achieve their full potential because the bridges between the various functions have not been built, or have been sabotaged. This then leads to the resolution of internal conflicts by office politics and inter-departmental power-play. Instead, you should play your part in the management team to ensure that intelligent and balanced discussion can take place, in which the views of all parties are equally respected and catered for, so that balanced decisions can be made.

The requirements for dealing with your boss and others senior to you are not dissimilar:

- clear but unemotive communication skills
- flexibility in accepting new ideas and taking direction,
- a willingness, nevertheless, to stand your ground and support your viewpoint, especially if you feel that not all the issues at stake have been fully explored, even if what you have to say may be unpopular,
- integrity in dealing with the issues (e.g. no exaggeration!) and other colleagues (e.g. no tales out of school – at least, not without having raised the issues with the relevant party first if it was appropriate),
- readiness to admit when you don't know all the answers, and then
- a willingness to seek help or advice.

In dealing with those who work for you, or who are otherwise junior in status to you, there is no reason why you should not adopt the same approach. In addition, you should also consistently seek to present an attitude that demonstrates:

- approachability
- fairness and consistency,
- knowledge of the key issues and a readiness to discuss them,
- an ability to admit you are wrong,
- a willingness to praise and acknowledge when things go right, and
- the ability to make clear and well-communicated decisions.

Whoever you have to deal with, above all your aim must be to

- generate and maintain mutual respect.

As with nearly all advice on management topics, most of these points are self-evident. The problem for many is that the lessons learned in theory tend to be forgotten in the heat of the moment, even by the most able. If you want to seek improvement in this area, try this exercise.

Useful Exercise: Interpersonal skills review

As you go home at the end of each day, review all of your major communications with those above, below and on the same level of seniority as you. Check these communications against the lists above. Even the most experienced and well-practised managers will regularly find there are occasions when they wish they could start some of the discussions of the day again. Learn from this self-analysis, because that is the best way to improve. If you regret some of the things you have said, why not go back tomorrow and correct that false impression, apologise for the ill-chosen comment, or clarify the inconclusive statement? Not only will this improve your performance of the moment, you will also improve your relationships for the future.

11

'In dealing with those who work for you . . . you should seek to present an attitude that demonstrates an ability to admit you are wrong.'

However skilled you are at dealing with your own colleagues, you will invariably come across problem people from time to time. We shall look at some of these, and how to deal with them, in the last section of this book.

3   Administration and the
Sales Office

Dealing with your field-sales force is perhaps the most obvious area where sound interpersonal skills will be vital. Because most sales managers have themselves been salesmen or women, they start off with the natural advantage of having a much closer understanding of what is required in the field. First-hand and immediate experience of the sales office, however, might be less common.

Nevertheless, having a happy, dedicated and well-organised 'inside' sales team is vital for any manager who seeks success. There is no point in having the best products in the world, sold by the best sales team you could ever wish to hope for, if you are let down by weak staff back home. If only by sheer geographical separation, it can be all too easy for inside staff to fail to understand the vital importance of providing the slickest and most enthusiastic possible back-up and service to your precious customers outside.

- Time spent with your sales office early on during your new appointment is rarely wasted.

- Time spent in the sales office regularly thereafter will also pay rich dividends.

Apart from distance from the customer, one of the problems for the sales-office team is that, rather than controlling their own time internally, they are largely controlled by the demands of their customers outside in the market-place. Their minute-by-minute

14

tasks are to answer telephones, enquiries and complaints, to organise the processing and perhaps despatch of orders, service back-up, and so on. In a badly run office, these demands can become a headless monster out of control. Your job must therefore be to:

- analyse the department's roles,

- then set priorities

- assign the work-load accordingly, and

- specify exactly what has to be done, by whom and when.

Sales-office manual

Although the need is self-evident from the above, very few sales offices actually have (or use) a *standard operating procedure* or sales-office manual. One of your earliest tasks must be to ensure that one is created, and used. Otherwise, you may well find that some of the more important decisions, such as applying discounts or offering special terms, are either being taken by staff who are far too junior to carry that level of responsibility, or are not being taken at all.

Often, you will find that office procedures have never been written down. This can be dangerous, especially if you should ever lose the few people in your organisation who *do* know the full detail of how things are meant to operate, with all the special exceptions that their experience has told them that they need to be aware of. Such people can also exercise a quite unbalanced sense of power and influence, out of keeping with either their authority or their skills. These longer-serving sales officers will know that a new sales manager cannot be expected to have all the necessary local knowledge of their specialist area to start with. They may also see that it is in their best interests never to let their manager acquire it. Not writing procedures down just prolongs this possible tyranny, under which senior decisions are taken far too low down the tree.

Specify therefore who has the responsibility for offering special discounts and accepting the credit-worthiness of new or even existing customers. Almost certainly it should be you. State what standards of response time you and, more importantly, your customers, are prepared to accept. Write down the complete procedure associated with taking enquiries, making quotations, processing orders, and so on. Decide who should keep which records and spell out how they should be used, and by whom.

The chances are that this sort of discipline will be met with wide-eyed wonder, but if you don't set the rules, who will? If such a manual does not exist already, recognise the change in operating-culture that you will have instituted. Accordingly, do not expect your instructions to be followed to the letter without a clear understanding being passed on as to why these changes are necessary, and how they are to be implemented. That means spending time on sales-office training. You will find it to be time well spent.

Sales-office support

During your early survey of the sales office, ask yourself what the sales-office team can do to help the sales force bring in more business. Properly trained, your inside sales team can help enormously. For example, they should be ringing up customers proactively to suggest that, from a study of the office records, the customer needs to reorder soon, or have a service visit. They can also spend time profitably ensuring that the customer is happy with his last delivery. Make sure that all calls are logged, and that your sales force is kept fully up to date with their calls. There is nothing worse for a salesman than to visit a customer unaware of what the office back at base has said or done – as you will surely know from past experience.

The measure of a well-run sales office is the attention paid to detail. You can never be sure that this is being given if you never check up. As with managing any other function, you will soon find that nearly every instruction you give will need to be checked. It is not that people are inherently lazy or uninterested, but rather that your staff's time-scales and standards cannot automatically be yours. In any event, there are enough distractions in most sales offices to provide a ready excuse for why matters that you hold as being important have not been executed as you would have wished. And if you find that things *have* been done just as you would want, don't forget to offer your appreciation or congratulations. There is nothing worse than working for an unappreciative boss!

4 Statistics and the Computer

In the good old (bad old) days, sales managers may well have believed that they, like salesmen, were born and not made. They may also have felt so confident of their innate skills that they had no great need to review detailed sales statistics and other related indicators of performance. Perhaps it is possible they did not need to, or even were not expected to. Just as likely, the figures were probably not even available.

Today, you will know that this should not be the case. The problem now is to decide, from the myriad statistics that are produced by zealous computer staff or accountants, what you need to know and how to use this information profitably. As time progresses, increasing numbers of sales forces will have their own portable computers, but you will still need to review what information they need and how they can derive the maximum benefit from it.

We shall look later at the detail of the records which your own sales staff might be expected to provide. At this stage, let us consider the two basic and over-riding questions which *you* need to answer from all the information you obtain.

- Are you on track with your performance to date?

If not, where do the problems lie and what are you going to do about them?

- What are you going to forecast for the next budgeting periods?

To answer these questions, the raw data that you need to measure should include:

enquiries,

their conversion rate to orders,

sales out of the door,

the profit margins (or sales contribution) generated by those sales;

each compared with your sales plan and sales target. Further, in order to manage your team's efforts in generating enquiries and converting them into orders, you will also want to monitor:

call rates, and perhaps even the duration of each visit,

the time spent on 'non-sales' activities such as administration and planning, training, sales conferences and even market research, together with

expenses and perhaps mileage driven.

We shall look at all these parameters in more detail later. First, there are three broader considerations.

- How often should all this information be reviewed?

A daily review may well be important, but in many businesses it will hardly be statistically valid in terms of providing longer-term indicators. You may therefore well decide that a weekly over-view would be more relevant, with special treatment perhaps for more detailed analysis on a monthly or quarterly basis.

- How will you judge whether your sales activities are going to plan? What are you going to compare your sales and operating data with?

The obvious comparison is with your budgeted targets, as already suggested, but it can also be invaluable to compare results with past performance. You might choose to compare the previous weeks, months or quarters, but don't forget to take into account any seasonal or cyclical factors that may affect your business such as holidays, customers' financial years or the weather. Accordingly, you will also want to look at the figures in preceding years – both for the period in question and cumulatively for each year. Figure 2 suggests how you might present this quickly and conveniently.

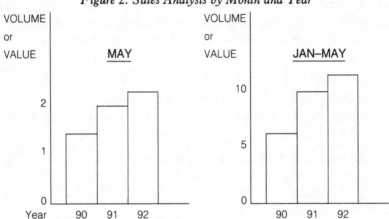

Figure 2: Sales Analysis by Month and Year

- How best should you analyse the details of your sales performance? How should you break down the available information?

Clearly, you need an analysis by sales person and region, and you will also want to monitor your major customers (say the top 20 per cent which, in many businesses, will account for the great majority of your sales: Pareto's Law suggests 80 per cent). But most probably you will also want to derive two other analyses:

a breakdown of performance by product (or product group), which will not only help your manufacturing colleagues in planning ahead, but will also be essential for planning your own sales and new-product planning strategy,

an analysis of sales by end-user market or application, so that you can plan your sales strategy and apply published trends for these sectors to your subsequent forecasting.

Beyond these traditional elements of data, there are also at least three others you will wish to record regularly:

market share (including imports into your home market perhaps), and movements in your major competitors' shares if at all possible, gauged from your sales teams' visit reports,

lost business analysis, indicating value and reason, which needs to be supplemented with an action list to recover the lost business next time, and

complaints analysis, again with some quantification of reparations made (such as credit notes or replacement goods), and of course an action list to avoid any repeat.

You may well feel that you are too busy to benefit from the study of this type of information, but it is only through the analysis of such indicators that you can judge what is happening to your business and the markets you serve. If the information is not available to you, your job will be that much more difficult, so you should insist upon having it. Even if your company does not feel it is appropriate, you can be assured that your more successful competitors will.

If it is relevant for your business, you will also want to record and analyse

stock availability (noting that 100 per cent availability is almost certainly cost-inefficient), and projected needs,

delivery performance against original promises,

21

profit generated by customer, market, salesman and territory,

product consumption of regular customers, so you know when they are likely to reorder,

response rates to mail shots, advertising and other specific promotional initiatives.

In reviewing this sort of data, you need to ensure that the information required is recorded in an appropriate format with a system for coding markets or products that suits *you*, rather than just your production or finance colleagues, for example. You may also need to ensure that your records are not wastefully duplicated.

Useful Exercise: Record duplication

Find out who else records the information of interest to you, especially in the finance and production departments. If it is not in the format which you want, accept a compromise if you have to. (You might also ask what *other* information they have, which you may like to see regularly!)

Then decide who should collate and disseminate it – for everyone. It should not matter who does it, as long as it is done well without errors or omissions, and promptly.

Data presentation

Having organised the data you need to run your team, you need to decide how you want it presented, so that you can use it efficiently. As a manager, you may well not need to know every minute detail. Here are some short cuts:

● **Report by exception.** Concentrate only on those items which do *not* meet your expectations or budget plan.

- **Report by variance.** Concentrate on the most significant variances, and ensure you understand why they have arisen. It could be that there is a simple coding error, for example, or it might rather be explained by some new and significant competitor activity, which forms a pattern when you have the broad over-view that your sales team might not yet have noticed.

- **Report on trends.** Computerised graphic packages for even the simplest and lowest-budget computers have taken much of the drudgery out of trend analysis, so make the best possible use of the enormous advantage our predecessors never enjoyed. Visual presentation of the information, by using pie charts, bar charts and graphs, can make comparisons of data very much easier. If you need to view longer-term trends, consider using moving averages plotted graphically against time.

Useful Exercise: Moving average trend-analysis

This is an invaluable method of looking at trends, whether monthly, quarterly or annually, where there are significant fluctuations in the shorter term which can mask the longer-term influence. A simple graph of actual sales against time may show large variations each period, but by plotting the *moving average*, these variations can be smoothed out and the underlying trend exposed.

To plot a moving quarterly (i.e. three months) average, add up the sales for the first three months of last year, say, and make this sum the first point on your graph. For the next point, subtract the first month's figure (January) and add the fourth (April). For the next, take this last figure, subtract the second month (February) and add the fifth (May), and so on. Note that every point you plot still covers three months' sales, but the period moves forward one month each time. A dip in the graph naturally indicates a declining trend, while a rise shows an improving trend. Figure 3 shows what your graph may look like.

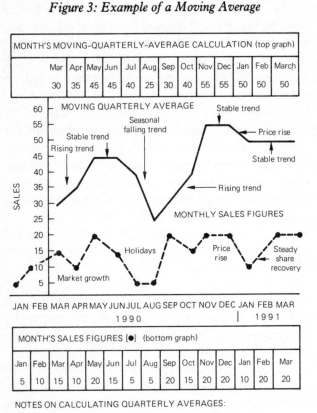

Figure 3: Example of a Moving Average

MONTH'S MOVING-QUARTERLY-AVERAGE CALCULATION (top graph)												
	Mar	Apr	May	Jun	Jul	Aug	Sep	Oct	Nov	Dec	Jan	Feb	March
	30	35	45	45	40	25	30	40	55	55	50	50	50

MONTH'S SALES FIGURES [●] (bottom graph)												
Jan	Feb	Mar	Apr	May	Jun	Jul	Aug	Sep	Oct	Nov	Dec	Jan	Feb	Mar
5	10	15	10	20	15	5	5	20	15	20	20	10	20	20

NOTES ON CALCULATING QUARTERLY AVERAGES:

March average = sum of sales for January, Feburary and March.
April average = March quarterly average minus January plus April sales.

Note that exceptional sales in any given month will give a rising trend for the next two months' moving average but, without another big sales month, the fourth month will show a correspondingly large dip as the effect of the 'big' month is removed. For longer time-scales, a moving *annual* total (known by statisticians as a 'MAT') of monthly figures may be more appropriate for your needs.

Moving averages can help in other ways. For example, they can also be used to track economic indicators which may affect your company's particular product sales, such as nationwide housing starts, steel production, new car registrations, etc. You can then check the correlation with your product sales, demonstrating any lead or lag. This will not only help you forecast future sales, but also indicate when you are performing particularly well or badly against the indicator you have chosen.

You can also combine a plot of moving average annual sales totals with monthly and cumulative sales, to produce the so-called *Z-chart*. The top of the 'Z' is the moving annual average, the diagonal is the plot of cumulative sales over the year, while the base of the 'Z' is the plot of each month's sales. In one diagram you can see the monthly and cumulative sales and the trend against the previous year. If you then plot your target sales in the same format, you can see at a glance exactly how you are performing against your original plan.

Computers

Computers can offer major benefits to the sales manager. They will handle your enquiry and order administration, sharpen your customer service and field-sales efforts, focus your direct marketing activities, assist your general marketing support, tighten up your sales-team control and add muscle to your planning.

Apart from helping to produce **graphics**, e.g. for planning or sales monitoring exercises such as those described above, or sharpening your presentations to customers, there are three other most important software packages with which you should become familiar:

Word-processing

Spreadsheets

Data bases.

With these simple tools you can target sales efforts, monitor new opportunities, build customer loyalty, maximise your cross-selling power, allocate your sales and distribution resources with maximum efficiency and forecast more precisely. How you use the computer will largely depend on your vision and experience, but

'Computers can offer major benefits to the sales manager.'

you will find that professional help is available from many sources if you need it.

The most popular use of smaller computers is still **word-processing**, which allows standard letters and quotations to be produced in bulk and yet be personalised. This immediately offers you the chance to attain a finished quality which may be impossible with individually written letters of a standard nature. It also opens up a realm of new opportunities for pain-free mail shots which many smaller offices would once never have dreamed of. These can be used for promoting special offers or new product-development launches, issuing updated stock lists, amending prices, thanking customers for their order and soliciting the next, arranging a customer follow-up, etc. Such technology also paves the way for the electronic transmission of mail and messaging, which may well herald the paperless office sooner than many people think.

In order to produce customised letters, you will soon find the need for the second essential piece of software: a **data base** system. This allows you to code contacts and customers, for example, by job description or purchasing authority, geographic location, account size and potential, business type, market sector, product usage, growth potential and even the best time of day or month to call. The key to all this is how you choose to code the fields that make up your data base. This will naturally require a clear decision by you, at an early stage, of what use you are going to make of this information. You will also need to make sure that the information you need is available, and decide who is going to collect it.

You can also use data bases for much more sophisticated analysis, which can help run a whole business if you want. Apart from allowing you to code and sort customers, you can analyse product performance, competitors, sales-team visit-plans and performance, sales costs, service histories, etc. Relational data bases will let you merge several different data bases and analyse related features at one go. All you need is practice and imagination and there are many types of proprietary software to meet specific needs if you prefer not to create the necessary package yourself.

The third essential piece of software is particularly important for planning purposes: the **spreadsheet**. At its simplest, it can ease the dread of budgeting. A simple change to one number is automatically calculated across the rows and down the columns of your plan without further effort. This means not only that you can take into account last-minute changes in sales forecasts, expenses, products, promotion, prices, costs, discounts or whatever; you can also play 'what if?' games. With little added sophistication, the effects of theoretical changes to your product, promotion, pricing, call rates or sales coverage can all immediately be revealed, according to the mathematical model you choose to set up.

Useful Exercise: Getting started with computers

For those who feel that the world of computing has either not reached them or left them behind, there may be some natural trepidation in starting now. On the other hand, how can you afford to forgo the huge benefits that computers bring?

The secret is to find a colleague, a consultant or even a friend, to support you. Then draw up a list of realistic requirements that you feel your department has. If the final list appears to be rather ambitious, prioritise your needs into 'must haves' and 'would like'. The second category can wait for a while.

You need to buy three components, all of which must be mutually compatible:

first, the **software** to handle these tasks,

then some **hardware** to run the software on,

and finally some means of reproducing the results, such as a **printer**.

Now decide who you want to operate this equipment (making a mental reservation that you will (must) force yourself to learn how to operate it, at least at a basic level) and estimate how much benefit you think the users might obtain, so you can decide the budget you can realistically ask for. Experience shows that it is probably unwise to budget for manpower

---

28

savings, at least initially. Your initial choice of equipment will almost certainly need to be upgraded within one to three years. The size of your operation will determine how much you need to spend, but you can do very well at the earliest stages with less than £2,000 at the time of writing. Note that while cheaper solutions may be somewhat limited, their greater simplicity may well make them much easier to learn and understand.

At last it is time to go shopping. Armed with your list of requirements, talk to as many suppliers as you possibly can. Establish what level of training and support they (not someone else) can offer and be sure to ask for some references of satisfied customers who have similar needs. You must follow these up. If you cannot find any similar users in your area, be very cautious. Make friends with fellow users: they may be of incalculable assistance once you are started. If your ambitions for your new system are high, make sure that what you buy can be upgraded later, unless you are happy to consider starting all over again in a more sophisticated manner once you have learned the basics.

When you have your equipment installed, there are two key rules:

- Involve as many of your department as possible.

Ideally, your team should have been involved from the beginning. Not everyone will have the same aptitude and inclination, but you will almost certainly be pleasantly surprised how quickly many will become immersed in an absorbing and rewarding activity. Allow people time to 'play'; there is little you can do to damage most equipment and familiarity breeds content.

- Do not be too ambitious to start with.

Set yourself just one task initially, such as learning the word-processor functions (once started, most secretaries won't want to revert to their typewriters), or entering your data base of customers and prospects, or setting up a spreadsheet for next year's sales plan.

Very soon, you will wonder how you ever managed to do without your purchase. Those colleagues who are not yet computerised will surely be envious, however sceptical they were to start with.

If you already have some computing facilities within your own company, you need to be sure that, having specified your needs, whatever you do next will be compatible with the equipment you already have.

In doing this, you may well find yourself in the vanguard of specifying a total IT (information technology) strategy for your company. This needs specialised help, but you will gain much credit from your senior management for proposing a company-wide solution.

Once started with implementing computerisation in your sales office, you are well on the way to additional rich prizes that are limited only by imagination and, let it be said, budget. In due course, orders can be entered from the telephone with automatic stock-allocation, pricing and delivery, without further effort. Bad debtors can be highlighted automatically and payment demands sent accordingly. You may well wish to issue portable computers to all your sales force for order entry, customer record or stock-interrogation from their customers' premises, electronic mail-messaging and so on. With networking, personal work-stations can 'talk' to each other. With Electronic Data Interchange, your customers can instruct their computers to order goods or services from your company, via your computer, without any human intervention.

All computerisation needs is to get started, some desire to make it happen and a willingness to invest in the future – which is fast becoming the present.

5   Sales Planning

A typical sales person, with car and expenses, probably costs at least as much as twice your salary. Multiply that by the size of your team and you have a very expensive asset. No effort must be spared therefore to make the very most of this costly resource. In order to do this, whatever the sophistication of your operation, sound planning will provide the key. While a computer can certainly help in this, it is not essential. Your prime job must be to make the most of your sales team, with or without computer assistance.

We shall look at various aspects of planning in detail throughout this book, but if you are new to sales management, or new to your business, you might just try answering the following check-list first:

Figure 4: Planning Check-list

Market Mission

- What do our customers and prospects need, and want, to buy,
- what are we going to sell?

The Prospects

- Who are we going to sell to,
- where are they,
- how are we going to sell to them,
- what is this going to cost us?

The Proposition

- Why should customers want to buy from us,

- when are they going to buy from us,

- how much are they going to buy from us

- who is our competition and how are we going to compete,

- what are we going to charge,

- when are we going to be paid?

The Method

- How many sales people do we need, where,

- what skills and training do they need,

- how are we going to reward and motivate them,

- how *should* they spend their time,

- how are we going to know how they are *actually* spending their time?

Support

- What stocks do we need, and what can we afford,

- do we also need distributors, agents or telesales help,

- what administrative back-up do we need,

- what technical or after-sales back-up do we need?

Promotion

- How are our customers going to know what we have to offer,

- how are we going to be sure we get all the enquiries of interest to us,

- how are we going to qualify each enquiry to make sure that each one *is* of interest to us?

32

The Results

- How much profit are we going to make,
- how will we know whether we will meet our plan,
- what will we do if our plan goes wrong?

Before you were promoted to your job as sales manager, you might well have thought that an intuitive sensitivity to customers' needs, together with a deep knowledge of sales techniques, the market-place and the product, would be sufficient for you to lead a successful sales team.

The intention of this Introduction is to suggest that much more is needed. In short, sales also have to be managed.

We look at the components of sales management, and the duties of a sales manager, in the next section.

II

WHAT A SALES MANAGER DOES

'Chance does nothing that has not been prepared beforehand.'
Alexis de Tocqueville

6 Key Requirements

The Introduction to this book confirmed that sales management is very different from selling. It is worth exploring in more detail just how different, by looking at the component duties of a sales manager. What does a sales manager have to do?

1) **Selection, recruitment and appointment.** Yes, you *can* have a choice of the personnel in your team. If you have inherited a team who are all star performers, you are exceptionally lucky. If you have not, you must consider making some changes.

2) **Training and development.** Training is a task that never ends. Before you make personnel changes, be sure that your poorer performers have indeed been given a fair chance. Ask when they last had any formal training, and assess whether they are capable of redemption. If they are, then train as if there was no tomorrow (which indeed there might not otherwise be). If they are beyond help, find some new blood. Don't forget your own training needs: you owe it to yourself, your team and, of course, your company.

3) **Organisation and planning.** A well-trained team now deserves an organisation that meets the requirements of both your company and its market-place. Organisations should be planned, rather than just allowed to happen. You have a very expensive asset under your control, and control is what it needs.

4) **Reporting controls and leadership.** A team without objectives to aim for, controls to ensure that these objectives are met and a purposeful sense of direction, isn't a team. A successful team is

one that knows clearly and unambiguously what the objectives are, understands how these objectives are to be achieved, and receives regular feedback of how performance in practice compares with the targets that have been agreed.

5) Motivation and reward. We all need encouragement and motivation, and sales people perhaps more than most. Rewards don't have to be just monetary, and sometimes are best when they're not. Where the rewards are financial, do you set reasonable targets that are measurable? And are the rewards cost-effective?

6) Forecasting and budgets. Better sales managers not only set realistic but aggressive sales targets, they also forecast accurately. This may be easier said than done, but someone has to do it, and who better than the sales manager? You don't want to accept targets handed down from on high, do you? Or to accept a 'fag-packet' calculation done at a moment's notice!

In any company, the specific duties and responsibilities of a sales manager will vary, but the core requirements listed above will invariably be the same. It is usual to see these duties covered in a job description, so that there is no misunderstanding. Just in case *you* don't have one, an example is shown in Figure 5. You will see it relates to a small company, so this particular post reports direct to the managing director. You will also see that the MD has made it clear that the responsibility for key accounts and export sales has been retained by him. Nevertheless, you will note that all the key duties described above have been included.

Figure 5: Job description

SALES MANAGER

Responsible to: The Managing Director

Reporting to this position: UK Area Sales Representatives
UK Sales Administration Staff

Scope of action:

All sales activities of the Company excluding nominated sales to specific customers and markets retained by the Managing Director.

Key tasks:

1. To promote the Company and its products to its best advantage under the guidance of the Managing Director and other senior officers.

2. To meet agreed sales targets for the Company's products on a regular basis at budgeted price levels or better.

3. To assist in the preparation of the annual Sales Budget, the setting of detailed sales targets and the monitoring of results.

4. The speedy and efficient administration of enquiries, orders and other sales documents, together with enquiry, order and sales statistics.

5. The identification, development and promotion of new products and new markets.

Other duties:

1. The selection, training and monitoring of performance of internal and external sales staff.

2. The direction of day-to-day sales activities including quotations, prospecting, order receipt, invoicing, market development, product development, complaints handling, etc.

3. The analysis of company and market data related to the sale of the Company's products and the preparation of the sales plans arising.

4. Assistance with the preparation and the execution of the Company's promotional and advertising activities.

5. Assistance with the setting of pricing targets and strategy together with their direct implementation. The co-ordination of all sales-related matters with other functions in the Company as directed by the Managing Director.

6. Control of the Company's terms and conditions of sale and the monitoring of debtors and collection.

7. The recommendation and monitoring of stock levels in order to meet market demands.

8. To monitor and record changes in market share, competitor pricing, the quality of competitors' service, new products and market development by competitors etc.

We shall now look at each of the above sets of duties separately, in more detail. Selling is not a science, there are too many uncertain variables. You may therefore prefer to say it is an art. However, all art-forms need discipline and a sense of structure to succeed. This is the central theme of the next section.

7 Selection, Recruitment and Appointment

'It is the mark of a good action that it appears inevitable in retrospect.'
R. L. Stevenson

The need to have the very best sales team possible is self-evident. The most successful companies with the best products in the market-place will rightly claim that they can only maintain their dominant position if they also have the very best representation possible. Equally, those companies who *cannot* claim to be the best in their sector will surely state, with perfect logic, that *their* need is accordingly even greater.

Either way, whatever your company's position, you should seek to have the best team you can. Training is an integral part of this, but the first job is to make sure that you have the right raw material. If you do not think you have people capable of being the best, do not be shy in making some changes. Second-best is neither good enough for you, nor for your employer. It is certainly not good enough for your customers.

Recruitment planning

Most successful companies set great store by their recruitment policies, which are invariably systematic and well thought through. They pay specific attention to the detail of each job to be filled, and the qualities required, well before they set out to recruit. Further, they do not prejudice these requirements for short-term expediency. They manage the selection process tightly, even if they employ outside consultants to assist, and they monitor the results assiduously. You will want to do the same.

Conversely, second-rate companies are often run by second-rate managers, who will often recruit third-rate staff (if only to protect themselves from competition, perhaps).

A major mistake in recruitment is to mould a job around the person or people you have in mind.

- Any job you recruit for should be moulded around the *company's* overall needs, not the candidate's.

Companies who fit jobs around the available personnel end up with a patchwork quilt of an organisation. This is a sure-fire route to not even having an organisation.

There are two key steps that need to be taken before proceeding further.

- Agree on a **job specification**.

What is the post to be called and who does it report to? What is the scope of the post's responsibilities and what limits are there in any decision-making authority? What are the key objectives and how will success be measured? Who else will the holder of this post need to work with in your organisation and are there any areas of potential conflict internally? What resources does the post command and are there any particular points to note about the working environment (e.g. off-shore, overseas, building sites, etc)? How senior is the post and what rewards and conditions of employment does it justify? Smart employers will also probably wish to highlight subsequent career progression opportunities. This last can be vital, not only in ensuring a longer-term management succession policy, but also in establishing the next requirement in the planning stage:

- Create a **candidate profile**.

Determine what skills, abilities and experience are essential for the job specification you have just outlined, without which the duties of the post could not be fulfilled. Then decide the other qualities which would be an additional bonus if you can find them, *but are not essential*. Be sure to distinguish accurately between the two. If you end up by specifying a paragon of all virtues, you will find that the post is impossible to fill.

Decide, for example, whether specific technical expertise or product application experience is necessary in advance, or whether relevant training can be provided, if required. Past experience in these areas is rarely as important as intelligence and personality. If you think you need to specify age-range, geographic location or future career potential, do so – but remember these considerations are rarely as critical as fundamental sales ability and a results-oriented personality. Note also that it is illegal in nearly all situations to discriminate in terms of race or gender.

Finding candidates

Only when you have drawn up the specifications for the job and the candidate is it appropriate to decide how and where you are going to find your successful candidate. It is nearly always good practice to advertise the post internally, even if you think there is little chance of finding an acceptable candidate within your own organisation. First, you may be surprised at the hidden talents which some of your own colleagues will possess; second, you will reinforce the feeling in your company that all employees are part of a genuine team, where merit and future potential can and will be recognised.

Interviewing internal candidates also gives your team the chance to practise their presentational skills. Some managers may balk at this, feeling that developing the interview skills of their own employees can only be to the company's disadvantage. In fact, experience shows that this is a very narrow-minded and short-term outlook. Further, if you have dissatisfied colleagues, you have a formal opportunity to find this out before they find alternative employment, rather than afterwards. A good interview

'Note that it is illegal in nearly all situations to discriminate in terms of race or gender.'

will provide a golden chance to explore discontent before the damage is irreparable. If you have colleagues with unrealistic aspirations, again it is better to give them an opportunity to come to terms with this sooner rather than later. If, conversely, you have a genius on your hands, it must be to your advantage to highlight the opportunities within your organisation, rather than outside, by demonstrating your commitment to recruitment from within wherever possible.

Assuming that you do wish to recruit from outside the company, or at least have the opportunity to consider outside candidates in competition with those inside the organisation, there are two basic methods:

Direct recruitment. This method has the advantage that you are in full control throughout the whole recruitment process. It is very time-consuming, but it does save paying for outsiders to do the work. In a recent survey for Hoggett Bowes plc by Market and Opinion Research (MORI) in England, 44 per cent of personnel directors polled in larger companies in the north favoured this approach, but only 24 per cent in the south.

External recruitment. The use of an outside specialist, if chosen carefully, can guarantee a more professional approach and can also offer initial anonymity if this is important to you. It can also be quicker, but many may feel that external assistance is more expensive.

Various services are available, ranging from just the placement of a recruitment advertisement, through initial screening by interview, to final appointment and even preparation of a contract of employment, if you should so wish. If you are seeking very special skills or experience, where the number of candidates may be limited, you might also consider the use of a 'headhunter' who will personally contact and then interview potential candidates identified by their own research. Some more traditional recruitment companies will also offer a similar but more limited search service, by trawling their data bases of past potential candidates who might meet your candidate profiles.

'You might also consider the use of a "headhunter" who will
personally contact and then interview potential candidates . . .'

Payment for external assistance may be by results only, on a so-called agency basis, or by a retainer fee for a full consultancy approach. According to the Hoggett Bowers survey mentioned above, agency methods are favoured by 28 per cent of larger companies in the south of England and 26 per cent in the north, while consultancy is preferred by a larger 42 per cent in the south but only 22 per cent in the north.

External recruitment

If you are tempted to use an outside agency or consultant, it pays to shop around. The total cost is normally based on a percentage of the successful applicant's first-year salary. This is often negotiable, although you will probably be told that it is not. It is not unusual to have the search fee payable in stages, the bulk of which you should endeavour to make payable only after a candidate has been found who is acceptable to you. You may also wish to agree at the outset on what is a mutually acceptable time-scale for finding suitable candidates. If the search fails to find the person you want, termination of the contract will then be that much easier. It is also normal to demand a partial refund if the candidate eventually selected proves to be unacceptable, or leaves you for any other reason within an agreed period such as six months.

You need to be careful in choosing your outside assistance. As even those who make their living this way will often acknowledge, there are still some in this field who have given their profession a bad name. Before employing such a service, establish who else they have worked for and ask in particular how candidates are found and approached. You should also discuss their organisation's code of ethics (which should normally forbid their approach to your own employees for other clients' searches) and you should not hesitate to take up some references. Above all, you should also meet anyone who may be involved with interviewing candidates for you, to make sure that they are fully briefed and can represent your interests in the manner you would wish them to.

There are two other points worth heeding in particular if you should choose to use an outside agency or consultant.

First, any recruitment company depends for its reputation on finding you good candidates – of course. Be cautious therefore that neither you nor they over-sell the job in order to attract good candidates. If there are 'warts' about the post (such as prolonged absence from home, or a tough business climate), it is better to ensure that prospective candidates are told this at the beginning of the selection process, rather than after they have joined you. You will only have to start the process all over again if a good candidate finds that he or she has been 'sold a pup' and leaves you. It doesn't do company morale much good either.

Secondly, recruitment companies must satisfy you that the good candidates whom they have found are indeed good. With the best will in the world, it seems that most agencies find it very difficult to avoid over-selling their candidates to their clients. If you do not think a candidate whom they have found meets your needs, say so. If you think you have only been told about the positive aspects of someone's candidacy, again say so.

Many agencies and consultants in this business complain that their clients regularly seek absolute perfection. This is indeed worth guarding against, or else you will never recruit anyone. However, one of the benefits of setting down a detailed and well-thought-out candidate specification is that it does force you to identify what is essential in a prospective candidate, and what is a bonus. If, before starting the search, your consultant has agreed with you on the list of mandatory skills and experience required by the post, you have every right to insist that these requirements are met. Remember: this chapter set out with the suggestion that you need the best sales team possible. Don't prejudice this goal now!

Poaching candidates

Many sales managers will be tempted, when seeking to fill a post, to make contact with potential applicants already known to them. This can be the cheapest method, and very effective, although it is of course limited in its scope of 'trawl' of possible candidates. All too often, however, this type of search means 'poaching' from the competition. This may be an attractive proposition, but there are some very significant disadvantages.

First, is it a realistic proposition to ask a sales person, who has spent his or her last job selling the opposition's products with competitive pride and enthusiasm, to go back into the same market-place and say with equal conviction and integrity that *your* products and service are now the ones that customers should be buying, and that previous recommendations were wrong? Under most circumstances, the answer is probably no.

There are also other considerations that can often make this an unappealing proposition. For example, what sort of candidates are you likely to attract? The very best sales people in your market will usually be recognised as such by their employers, who will often want to make counter-offers to retain them. This may be a desirable outcome for the individuals concerned, but it is unlikely to benefit you. Accordingly, those staff who do move from one competitor to another are, in practice, all too often only the second-best. They are also rarely very troubled by concepts of company loyalty. Is that what you want? Further, if you acquire a reputation in your business sector for poaching from your competitors, you may well find that the chances of your own staff being poached will also increase.

In all, recruitment from within an industry is not without its problems. Naturally, there are some advantages in recruiting from your competitors, and many companies appear to make a regular practice of doing so. However, the judgement of the net balance of opportunity is rarely favourable. Before you decide to poach from a competitor, therefore, be sure that you have not under-estimated the potential disadvantages outlined above.

Advertising

Advertising for candidates can be done by yourself, or by a specialist company such as described above who might also do the initial screening interviews for you. This can be a substantial benefit if you expect to receive a large number of replies, many of which may not actually meet your needs. Whoever is responsible for the advertising, whether it is an agency, a consultant or yourself, there are a number of key points to consider if you wish to ensure a good response:

- **Headline your advertisement with core essentials, such as the job title and location.** You might try some eye-catching phrase or graphic design, but in general such a gimmick is not to be recommended. ('See the world at our expense!' ran one advertisement for an export sales manager. That is hardly the best way to recruit an export professional who is going to *sell* for you, rather than just clock up miles in an aeroplane, and vast hotel expenses.)

- **If at all possible, specify the salary and whether there is a bonus or commission scheme.** If you really feel you cannot indicate the likely earnings potential, recognise that your response rate will be significantly curtailed (some would say by up to two-thirds). Don't be hesitant in highlighting any other benefits you can offer, but these should preferably be kept to the end of the advertisement as matters of detail.

- **Ensure that you give a brief but adequate description of the company, the market, the product and the opportunities these present, followed by the duties to be performed.** Note that good sales people will want to work for successful companies, run by able managers. Do not be hesitant in highlighting the strengths of your company therefore, and the career opportunities you can offer. If you do not wish to give your company's name, you are almost obliged to advertise under the name of an outside recruitment consultant or agency. Note that box numbers have a very bad reputation amongst candidates as being time-wasters, and possibly of dubious ethics. Response rates are accordingly very poor.

- **Specify the requirements of the post.** Refer back to your candidate specification and highlight the qualities which you consider to be essential. This takes space, and space costs money, but failure to specify requirements will surely result in having to wade through what may be a large response, composed largely of people who are not going to meet your needs. Nevertheless, do not be tempted to fall into the opposite trap of specifying too many needs. First, you may find your response rate is unnecessarily curtailed. Second, these needs will invariably become unquantifiable. Statements such as 'Able to work hard' and demands for 'a real sales professional' hardly help an advertisement; how many applicants are going to deny that they have those qualities?

- **Specify what candidates should do next to progress their application.** You may want them to ring a specified telephone number in the evening or over the weekend, but it is more usual to ask for a detailed curriculum vitae, highlighting career successes to date. The problem with this is that invariably you will not receive all the information you need, such as present earnings and availability. One solution is to invite candidates to fill in a company application form that will specify all the information you need. Note, however, that if you do this you will discourage some able applicants who will see such form-filling as indicative of an inflexible, bureaucratic company. You may well feel that a c.v., followed by a preliminary screening telephone call to those candidates who look most interesting, might be the better option.

  One other point: try to avoid asking candidates to send the applications to a personnel department. This is another indicator of a stodgy, bureaucratic company. Your interest in the appointment will be much more obvious if you can have applications sent to you, even if you forward them afterwards to your personnel team.

For more information on advertising in general, and what makes for a successful advertisement, see also under *Promotion* in the 'Marketing' section which follows this.

Interviewing

This is a specialist skill that is underrated in its demand for professionalism, although many excellent books and training films are available for self-help if you have not been professionally trained. There are a number of golden rules:

- **Make time to concentrate exclusively on the job in hand.** Do not permit any interruptions once the interview is in progress and clear your desk or interview table of all extraneous matter. While the interview is in progress, you must make the candidate feel that nothing else is more important – which should indeed be the case.

- **Before you start, assume nothing about the candidate and work hard at recognising (and then abandoning) your personal prejudices.** Don't let a regional accent, physical stature, or even choice of clothing put you off, unless you have genuine reason to believe that it will also put your customers off. Above all, don't feel you have to pick a candidate who is a clone of yourself or your background. The best teams are often characterised by their diversity, not their uniformity.

- **Put candidates at their ease.** You will learn far more from interviews this way than if you set out to attack them. However experienced the candidate, there is almost bound to be some element of nervousness. It seems traditional to ask about the candidate's journey as a means of starting the interview in a relaxed manner, but any other neutral topic of conversation is equally acceptable (and probably more welcome, as a change) as long as it is not allowed to become the dominant focus for the rest of the interview.

Figure 6: Interview Check-list – Sales Appointments

NAME: .... DATE 1) .... DATE 2) ....

REGION: .... SALES EXPERIENCE: .... YEARS

WHAT DISCOVERED ABOUT COMPANY?

COULD HAVE DISCOVERED MORE?

WHY INTERESTED IN VACANCY?

WHY LEFT PREVIOUS JOBS?

DEFINITE CAREER PATH FOLLOWED?

CHIEF MOTIVATORS?

MANAGEMENT AMBITIONS?

SALES SKILLS?

MARKETING SKILLS?

NUMERATE?

TECHNICAL KNOWLEDGE?

MARKET KNOWLEDGE?

SPECIFIC SKILLS?

HEALTH

CLEAN LICENCE?

DOMESTIC CIRCUMSTANCES?

ABSENCE FROM HOME?

AVAILABILITY?

SALARY?

BONUS?

PENSION SCHEMES?

CAR?

OUTSIDE INTERESTS?

NEWSPAPERS READ?

APPEARANCE/PERSONALITY?

PHYSICAL?

FACIAL?

DRESS?

PRESENCE?

ARTICULATE?

MANNER?

DRIVE/ENTHUSIASM?

ENDURANCE?

EMPATHY?

INITIATIVE?

INTELLIGENCE?

ORGANISATION?

HONESTY?

ADMIN SKILLS?

LANGUAGES?

TRAINING NEEDS?

ADMITTED STRENGTHS?

ADMITTED WEAKNESSES/LIMITATIONS?

WHAT SORT OF PEOPLE DO YOU FIND DIFFICULT TO WORK WITH?

SURE OWN STRENGTHS SATISFY JOB DEMANDS?

SHORT-TERM ASPIRATIONS LIKELY TO BE MET?

LONG-TERM ASPIRATIONS LIKELY TO BE MET?

ASKED INTELLIGENT QUESTIONS?

EXPENSES:

QUESTIONS TO ASK NEXT TIME:

REFEREES:

Interviewers:

53

- **Do ask open-ended questions (starting Who? What? Why? When? How? Where?) that demand more than a straight 'yes' or 'no'.** Don't say 'We believe accurate record-keeping of customer details and visit reports is essential. Do you agree?', for example. A close-ended response which you thus invite, whether yes or no, is not very helpful. Instead, ask 'What are your ideas on record-keeping? How do *you* like to work?' Don't tell the candidate that you think product knowledge is a vital requirement of a salesman, but ask what *they* think the key skills are. Your objective should be for the candidate to do most of the talking, not you.

- **Challenge the answers given.** Ask for examples of *why* they felt their last post was the success that is being claimed; ask *how* their success was obtained; enquire *why* they are seeking alternative employment if they were so successful or, if it wasn't such a success, establish what the candidate thinks the reasons were. This all needs to be done unemotionally and objectively or the interview will become combative, but it does need to be done.

- **Keep to a pre-planned programme of questions and don't let a candidate side-track you.** In advance of your interview programme, draw up a check-list of all the points you want to cover. Then ask these of *every* candidate whom you choose to interview. Figure 6 may help you to draw up a list that meets your specific needs. If you find the candidate raises points that take you away from the ground you wish to explore, remember *you* are in charge. It is quite acceptable to note a point or question, remark that it is of interest and suggest that you come back to it later.

- **Give the candidate a chance to ask you questions.** Candidates' questions provide an excellent guide as to how serious each application really is. They also serve to highlight any matters which may concern your preferred candidate. You will need to address these concerns before you can be sure any offer which you make will be acceptable. For preference, you should note candidates' questions, as you should all their answers. A candidate who asks no questions, or irrelevant ones, is probably not for you. The ability to ask good questions is a key skill for any sales person.

- **Terminate the interview, succesful or otherwise, by expressing thanks for the candidate's interest and time, and make it clear when you expect to advise of the outcome.** Remember that not only are you interviewing candidates, they will also be interviewing you. You too therefore need to leave a good impression, whether or not you are likely to be offering an appointment. Even if they do not join you, who knows when you will meet them again? Unless you wish to suggest that your company is very mean, you will also ask the candidate to claim for any reasonable expenses they have incurred.

Useful Exercise: Interviewing skills

How good an interviewer are you? Few of us are as good as we would like to be, or believe ourselves to be. Good candidates are as quick to spot the amateur or downright poor interviewer (which can only reflect badly on your company) as you should be quick to select good candidates.

The secret is practice, but preferably when it doesn't matter. If you can, hire a closed-circuit television studio for a couple of hours and role-play with some trusted colleagues. The rules are simple. Agree a scenario and go through your regular routine. Then play back the recording and have both parties analyse it rigorously. What did the interviewee feel when you suddenly asked this, or didn't follow through on that? What pertinent secrets did you fail to uncover? How did your colleague feel about the balance of speaking and listening time between the two of you? Could you have phrased any of your questions better?

Success rates of interviews

You may well feel that interviews on their own are poor indicators of a candidate's likely suitability. This may be especially true if you have, yourself, ever been turned down for a job for which you felt you were eminently well suited! However, in a survey of 320 UK companies published in 1988 by the Institute of Manpower Studies, over 90 per cent claimed to use interviews for selection, along with c.v. checks and references, and 96 per cent of those using interviews claimed that these were a reliable predictor of success. You may think that this is a surprisingly good result. What are the alternatives?

You might consider using one or more of a large number of psychometric and specialised aptitude tests. Only 10 per cent of those polled in the above survey used such methods, which clearly require specialist and trained application and interpretation. Of this 10 per cent, only 30 per cent claimed that they were confident that these tests were a reliable predictor of trainability and only 19 per cent felt that they were a good indicator of personality. In my experience these figures are very low, but as with all matters in this field, measuring results suffers from the fact that any conclusions must be highly subjective.

Some companies like to take candidates away for a weekend of role-playing exercises, others rely on studies of candidates' handwriting, some even recruit on the basis of birth signs. You may well feel that these are even more uncertain methods than the traditional interview. In any event, short-listed candidates will need to know about you, your products and the company's philosophies, just as much as you will want to know about them, their past experiences (both good and bad) and future aspirations. Accordingly, perhaps it is not surprising that the interview is still the most popular recruitment method available.

Exploration

The core part of any interview will consist of a detailed review of the candidates' career-histories. Only by going through each job, noting the dates of appointment and leaving, can you be sure you haven't missed any 'black holes' which a candidate may prefer to skate over, such as dismissal. As a supplement to the interview check-list, Figure 7 provides a useful check-list of questions which you will need to ask for each post your candidate has held. (Don't forget that you will also want to check the detail of these answers when you take up references.)

Any comment your candidate makes that is relevant to the post you are seeking to fill must be probed. It could be talk of a previous boss who was 'unreasonable' (in what way? why? how did others cope? could you perhaps also expect to have the same difficulties if this person became an employee?), a job that was particularly well done (what made it such a success? who really was responsible? how did things turn out subsequently?) or a special situation that could confront your candidate in this post too.

Figure 7: Checklist for Candidate Exploration

Establish, for each job:

- when they joined,
- why they joined,
- what their duties were,
- who they reported to,
- what they earned on appointment, and
- final earnings,
- what was achieved in the post, and
- why they left.

If certain technical or linguistic skills are a basic requirement of the job, you must check them out. If you demand basic numerical skills, ask each candidate the same questions so that you can make comparisons. E.g. What is 15 per cent of 90? How did you work it out? (Possibilities include using a calculator; taking 10 per cent of 90 and adding half as much again, or even taking 10 per cent away from 15; or working it out long-hand. The first and last are possibly not acceptable to you.) If prospecting skills are important, ask how the candidate would find out who all the widget-users were in a given territory (by desk research, from trade directories in a library and old customer records; by field research of existing customers; etc.) If knowledge of a specific language is required which you do not speak, don't be shy! Have a sample letter or enquiry written in the language in question, translated for you by a professional, and then compare this with your candidate's efforts. You may be surprised at the results: my personal experience shows that the most fluent tend to be misleadingly modest; the least, the reverse.

You will also want to explore candidates' domestic circumstances. Some matters are none of your business, although you may well want to probe gently to see if there are any particularly strong religious or political viewpoints, for example, that could perhaps cloud good relationships between the candidate and prospective customers – or colleagues. If applicable, you must ask, for example, who takes the kids to school. Domestic duties such as this are an unacceptable, if time-honoured, way of reducing the effective working day of any sales person beyond reasonable measure. You might also ask how the candidate's partner feels about absence away from home in the evenings, if it is relevant. It is always better to establish such points before making an appointment rather than afterwards.

Underneath all this probing, it is important to recognise that you will, however subconsciously, want to sell your company and the job, just as recruitment consultants will be inclined to, as already mentioned. Equally, good candidates will also want to sell themselves to you. Nevertheless, the foundation of the interview must be mutual honesty. There is as little point selling candidates a job for which they are ill-suited as there is for candidates to pretend that they are what they really are not. The cost of making a wrong appointment can be very damaging to both parties. As it is not normally realistic to expect candidates to accept that they may have limitations, it does no harm to stress at the outset that it is in neither party's interests to pretend what is not true.

Selection

The final decision on whom you choose to appoint will require judgement, imagination, skill and, many would say, luck. As already indicated, some recruitment companies specialise in sales appointments and may well back up their judgement with specialist aptitude tests. As long as you are prepared to keep an open mind and learn from your mistakes, any additional aid is probably worth exploring.

In the end, however, it must be your judgement that counts. Some interviewers develop what they claim to be a special, intuitive sixth sense in selecting winners. If you know such people and their record is good, you will want to learn from them by matching your choice against theirs. With this in mind, there is much to be said for asking colleagues whose opinions you value to join you in the selection process. Apart from the benefits that you will gain from their assistance, this is a good opportunity to expose your candidates to other members of the company. It is also an excellent aid to team-building.

Some would argue that the selection process should be biased towards eliminating losers; others that you need rather to select winners. Both are right. The natural inclination however seems to be to look only for reasons why you should *not* recruit. This can be a very negative approach and may need to be resisted. Above all else, avoid basing your selection on prejudice or market gossip. Rather, concentrate on exploring the reality of the candidates in front of you.

On occasions, you may feel that the post you are offering will not be sufficiently attractive to tempt your favoured candidate. It pays to keep this possibility in mind at the beginning of your selection process, rather than face it at the end. You might therefore keep a balance sheet of the benefits and disadvantages which the post offers just in case of such problems. It mirrors the check that your favoured candidate will probably do. An example of such a balance sheet is given in Figure 8.

Another problem, which is bound to face you at one time or another, is the failure of any candidate to meet your mandatory

59

Figure 8: Job Comparison

NAME: _____ DATE: _____

	Definite benefits	Same benefit	No change	Some loss	Definite loss
Direct Money					
Car					
Profit share					
Other benefits					
Status					
Responsibilities People					
Company					
Financial					
Influence on others					
Influence from others					
Future potential Responsibilities					
Status					
Financial					
Job satisfaction					
Living style Family					
Standard					
Style					
Company image					
Team involvement					

requirements. The temptation is then to reduce the acceptance standards you have drawn up. This may, perhaps, be appropriate. Alternatively, you may feel that a probationary period will allow you to assess a high-risk candidate adequately before confirming the appointment. However, if you are really unsure whether to offer an appointment, it is almost certainly better not to; start the recruitment process again.

References

When terms are finally agreed to both parties' satisfaction and a starting date is set, you must take up references to check the basic information which the candidate has volunteered. You need to do this to confirm the qualifications and experience you have been told about, as well as to gain more subjective information concerning work ethics and attitudes. Note that reference-checking should be mandatory, preferably in person or by telephone, rather than by letter. Few people will commit themselves freely in writing and even personal contact needs careful handling.

First, make sure that the referees volunteered include the immediate past boss. When you make contact, introduce yourself and stress that you would like to seek a reference *in confidence*. Identify the post on offer, sketch out the responsibilities and any notable challenges that it holds, and then ask open-ended questions:

- When did X join you?

- What was the position?

- How successful would you say X was?

- What were the major achievements?

- Were there any areas where you were disappointed in X's performance?

- Why was this?

- Why did X leave you?

You also need to listen carefully to the answers: few people will actually say that X was a good-for-nothing rogue for example! If you have doubts, answers to the following can be very revealing indeed:

- Would you consider employing X again?

- In what capacity?

- What job would you say X would be best suited to?

Appointment

At last you are in a position to make the appointment. It is not unreasonable for a candidate to ask that you only take up references once an offer has been made formally. If this is the case, make your offer subject to suitable references. (In passing, you may also wish to make the appointment subject to a simple medical examination, which should be conducted by a doctor of *your* choosing who knows your requirements, rather than a doctor of the candidate's choice).

Note that an oral offer of employment is as binding as a written one, so be careful of what you say.

Figure 9 provides a basic check-list of what any standard contract of employment should cover. Because there are quite specific legal requirements for a contract of employment, you should obtain professional advice if you are in any doubt. In particular, whether by letter or standard form, you need to state the job title, specific duties and to whom the post reports (specified by job title, rather than individual name) and the starting date. All your company lawyer's concerns about trade secrets, employees' illness or other incapacity, etc., need to be included, but there is nothing wrong with a simple exchange of letters to get matters started. Simply write to the candidate enclosing a duplicate copy, outlining the post you are offering. Confirm the details you have agreed on and request that one copy be signed, dated and returned to you, if it is acceptable.

Figure 9: Principal Components of a Contract of Employment

- Name and address of employer.

- Employee's position (job title) and to whom this position reports.

- Date of commencement. If the appointment is an internal transfer, show that employment is continuous.

- Salary/wage, any specific regional allowance, and how payment is to be made (e.g. Monthly in arrears direct to a nominated bank account, by the last working day of each month).

- Other benefits, such as a car (and under what conditions), travelling expenses, medical or permanent health insurance, protective clothing, etc.

- Bonus or commission schemes, etc., and how paid.

- Official hours of work and place of work, or mobility, as relevant.

- Holidays and holiday pay.

- A satisfactory medical examination prior to commencement.

- Absence through sickness, sick pay and what should happen in the event of long-term incapacity or illness.

- Grievance procedure and disciplinary rules.

- Notice of termination, subject to the disciplinary code, etc. (Note that if the notice period is specified in 'months', this means calendar months in UK law. It is usual to make the period of notice the same, from either the employer or the employee, but this is not mandatory.)

- Notification of changes in personal circumstances, such as address.

- Draw attention to the company's Health and Safety at Work policy.

Other features

- Details of any training or probationary period.

- Restraint clauses. (Beware! Note that any restraint on an employee to exercise his or her professional skills, even in direct competition, is unlikely to be legally enforceable unless some reasonable payment in compensation is provided during the period of restraint.)

- Company secrets and their safeguard (including the ownership of any patents granted in the exercise of the employee's duties).

- Prohibition of any parallel employment (i.e. moonlighting).

- Removal costs, mortgage assistance, temporary accommodation, etc.

- Medical examination at regular intervals after appointment.

- Subscription to professional bodies, etc.

- Details of any company pension scheme (membership of which, in the UK, cannot now be made obligatory).

The salary should be mentioned, confirming how it is to be paid, how regularly it is to be paid, and how regularly it is to be reviewed. Include details of any bonus or commission schemes, specify official working hours and holidays and whether overtime is to be paid (presumably not for a sales person!), and indicate how allowable expenses will be reimbursed. A salesman needs to be mobile: if this is vital, you should consider making this an essential requirement.

If a company car is to be provided, you should specify under what circumstances it may be used (e.g. is company permission required to take it abroad? must it be returned immediately if – for any reason – the company should so demand? etc.). What costs of running, taxing and insuring the car will the company cover, and what will be the employee's responsibilities (including the payment of private motoring, garaging overnight or regular cleaning, notification of any accidents or legal proceedings, etc.)?

Specific mention must be made about termination of the contract and the notice required by either party. If you have an official company disciplinary code, you should refer to it and ensure that the new employee gets a copy.

Having gained your candidate's acceptance, you now need to prepare for his or her arrival.

8 Training and Development

'Only the mediocre are always at their best.'
Robbie Taylor, et al.

A manager's responsibility for training his or her staff covers not only new employees, but existing ones. The needs of both categories of people, different though they are, are often forgotten. One hopes that this is a little rarer in the case of new colleagues, if only because their needs are – or should be – that much more obvious. Nevertheless, in one survey conducted by Industrial Market Research Ltd in the UK, only 79 per cent of the companies surveyed admitted to training new sales recruits formally; thereafter, only 58 per cent periodically. This is clearly not an acceptable state of affairs.

Induction

The first days for anyone in a new company or post are critical. A well-organised and formally planned induction programme can excuse all sorts of problems which a company may unwittingly place in an employee's way later on. Handled badly, however, a disorganised start is rarely forgotten, or forgiven. If the starting date proposed coincides badly with other pressures on your time, you would do better to pick another starting date, when you can discharge your responsibilities properly, rather than muddle through.

A comprehensive induction programme for a new employee should include:

- A description of the company from the top (i.e. parent or holding company) down, its senior officers and their duties, something about the company's history and its overall business objectives.

- An outline of the commercial environment you operate in; your principal markets and customers, your competitors and, if relevant, your suppliers,

- A description of your products, services and special capabilities, which should include company brochures and product documentation,

- At least a brief review of your recent trading history and the latest published accounts, together with relevant aspects of the company's budget and long-range forecasts,

- An organisation chart and an introduction to all the key personnel. If it is not possible to meet everyone you would wish your new employee to meet immediately, keep a check-list to ensure that no one is missed out.

- A tour of the offices and factory sites, including lavatories, canteens and office facilities such as typing, photocopying, fax machines and so on. Don't forget the switchboard and reception.

In addition, you should have arranged in advance,

- An announcement internally (and probably externally) of the new appointment, with details of immediate past career history if the new person agrees, with a copy for the new employee on arrival if not before,

- Some visiting cards, and company credit cards if these are standard issue,

- A copy of the company's rules and regulations, which should preferably include copies of the disciplinary code, the sales-office manual (see earlier), and reporting procedures with working examples of visit reports, customer records and expense claims.

Your initial objective should be to give the new person an overview only. Allow plenty of time for questions and be sure that the overall atmosphere is positive, encouraging and honest. Be proud in what you have to show, but don't hide the bad news. It is much better to tell this straight at the beginning, rather than have your expensive new recruit find it out from someone else later.

Product familiarisation

For a new recruit, product training may well take some time. At the beginning, cover the broad picture only. You can get into the detail later. For example, companies will vary in their methodology for coding products, some being more logical and rational than others. If your product terminology is potentially confusing, then concentrate on the more important products and applications first. Avoid information-indigestion at all costs.

The best way to introduce the product range in detail is in the field, once the initial familiarisation is over. It is much easier to remember key points in the heat of live customer interaction than in an office, but make sure that this is done by accompanied visits. It is wrong, unreasonable and unfair to throw a new recruit into battle without an experienced colleague alongside, and for preference that colleague should, at least initially, be you or a trusted deputy.

Product knowledge

Detailed product-knowledge training is not something that should be aimed at new recruits only. It is something that even your most hardened professional sales people will need regular updates on. Complacency engendered by an approximate product familiarity can be dangerous; it may be losing you business and your sales team commission. Training therefore needs to be a regular event which all of your team should expect as of right. Remember, the most frequently voiced criticism of sales people by their customers is lack of product knowledge.

Acquiring this knowledge starts at a product's birth: the sales launch. As a sales professional yourself, you know that it is not just the features of a product that are important, but the benefits. Why was the product developed? Who for and what for? What else is available in the market and how are competitors' products to be countered? How is the price made up and what other products can be sold as an add-on?

Thereafter, this information needs regular updating. Not only that – if the product, its price or packaging are not right, it should be your sales force who alert you before failed sales targets do. This updating therefore needs two-way communication, and good communications need regular, formalised channels. You might therefore plan a product revision and updating session as a regular feature of your sales meetings, or even during your accompanied sales visits. In addition, or instead, you might prefer to do this at meetings specifically designed to focus on product knowledge and market reaction.

Sales and negotiating skills

You may feel that good sales people are born, but even if you do, professional skills still need to be trained. Even outstanding sportsmen and women, who have immense natural ability and talent, become world-beaters only with regular training. Ask any football or athletics coach! So also with a sales team.

A wise manager will always play to the strengths of a person in the team, and shield the weaknesses, but regular training gives you an opportunity to ensure that those strengths that exist are genuine and that the weaknesses are minimised. This is therefore a topic worth covering as regularly as product training.

How you establish the relative strengths and weaknesses of your people is covered in the *Appraisal* section later, but you will

'Professional skills need to be trained . . .'

probably already recognise that no one is perfect, least of all yourself. For this reason, it is important to consider your own role in training activities. By all means engage outside help in this area, but don't be too proud to involve yourself as well. Indeed, it is said that one of the best ways to learn something is to teach it. If you have the confidence and are prepared to learn some basic training skills, as any professional manager should, why don't *you* take a topic dear to your heart and run a short seminar for your staff? This is also an excellent means of building team spirit.

Market background

Regular briefing of what is going on in your market-places should also be included in your training schedules. We will discuss marketing relative to selling later, but suffice it to say here that good market intelligence and understanding is often the hallmark of a successful team. Your sales staff should be your eyes and ears in the market-place. To achieve this, your team must be aware of the issues so that the information they glean is acquired intelligently. Typical items should include who owns whom, who is in which markets and what their markets shares are, how busy those markets are, the size of each of the major customers and competitors, their financial performance, who has won what major contracts, and so on. It is clearly a subject that needs communication in both directions: from you to your team and vice versa.

Training summary

Figure 10 summarises the results of a survey in the UK on the most frequent training topics in various sizes of company, and it makes interesting reading. However, the training responsibilities of a sales manager cover a much wider range of activities than these. A 1988 survey by *Sales Direction Magazine* in the UK showed that training effort tends to be focused much too often on product knowledge, to the exclusion of negotiating skills, time-management and questioning/listening skills, for example. To these omissions one might add other skills which need to be trained, such as forecasting, developing account strategies and a basic knowledge of finance. Even 'sales skills' need to be broken down into components, such as planning, prospecting, making appointments, establishing customers' needs, giving persuasive presentations, handling objections, solving problems, closing, etc.

Figure 10: Ranking of Training Topics

TRAINING TOPIC	NUMBER OF EMPLOYEES				
	UP TO 100	101 to 500	501 to 1,000	OVER 1,000	ALL
PRODUCT KNOWLEDGE	85%	74%	80%	87%	78%
SALES SKILLS	65%	68%	70%	70%	69%
COMPETITOR KNOWLEDGE	35%	41%	58%	61%	47%
SALES ADMIN.	23%	36%	55%	35%	38%
REPORTING/FEEDBACK	38%	39%	30%	43%	38%
USER KNOWLEDGE	38%	28%	25%	26%	29%
COMPANY KNOWLEDGE	19%	26%	25%	17%	24%
MORE THAN ONE	92%	83%	90%	91%	87%

From *How British Industry Sells*, G. Brand & F. Suntook
(Industrial Market Research Limited).

Good training is rarely inexpensive – so it should always be cost-effective. Untargeted training in particular can be very wasteful. Here are some helpful guidelines:

- Ensure that the training you give meets not just the needs of your staff, but also the needs of your company and the goals you set.

- New skills acquired through training need to be reinforced in practice, or they will soon be lost. (There is little point in developing skills that are not going to be used!) One way to provide this reinforcement in practice can be to set new tasks or targets that will make specific use of these skills.

- Accordingly, it is worth remembering that training is more than just sending people on courses. Training can – and needs to – happen both on and off the job.

- Any training activity is incomplete without feedback from those being trained, together with a review of the training's effectiveness. Make sure that every hour spent training does genuinely contribute to your company's greater success.

- Keep a record of training sessions. This will serve as a useful reminder of needs. It may also allow you to claim for a training grant in some cases.

Useful Exercise: Training review

Survey everyone who works for you.

- What training sessions, internal and external, have they each participated in, run by whom, when?

- How was each course rated, what benefits were obtained and what follow-up on each topic is now needed?

- What other areas do your team feel that they need help with?

You should provide a check-list of all those items which you feel are essential skills, to jog your team's memories. You should then compare your team's assessment of their needs with your own view. We shall cover this aspect in more detail later, under *Appraisals*.

Keep this data updated and regularly review sales performance against past training activity and future needs. Be careful to interpret those training needs claimed by your staff. Your own view in the end may well be more accurate! You will, more than probably, find some people who are 'perpetual students' of training sessions, and others who are congenitally shy.

---

9 Organisation and Planning

'Everything tends to a natural state of disorder.'
The Second Law of Thermodynamics.

'Good order is the foundation of all things.'
Edmund Burke

If you have read so far, you will already have seen that analysis, organisation and planning are essential requirements of a professional manager, especially in the field of selling. The first organisational consideration is the size of your sales team and its disposition. You probably inherited your sales team and the division of the overall territory into regions, for example, but you don't have to keep things that way.

For example, how many sales staff do you need? Who do they call on, why, and how often? What proportion of the calls should you expect to produce genuine enquiries and how many of these should be converted into orders? What work-load does all this imply, and what sales results can you expect from this effort? How are journey plans made, and could they be more effective and efficient?

Sales-force size

The optimum size of a sales force is rarely calculated with any degree of discipline. This is astonishing given the cost. One certainly would not expect a factory manager to get away with such sloppiness in determining the size of his work-force! However, any method you use will need careful attention to detail.

Sizes of sales teams vary considerably. Surveys in the UK show that smaller companies (up to 100 employees or £1 million sales) typically employ about five in their sales forces, according to work by Industrial Market Research and, separately, *Sales Direction Magazine*, while larger companies have a median size of sales team of about twenty. Companies employing over 1,000, or with sales over £100 million, may have field-sales forces of well over fifty, especially those in the repeat industrial or consumer fields, while sales teams of many hundreds – and even thousands – are not unknown in the financial services sector. These surveys demonstrate how variable the numbers employed in a sales team can be. They also highlight how realistic and practicable it is to be really quite flexible in determining the optimum size.

One way to calculate you own optimum number of field-sales people is to establish the number of customers and prospects your company must call upon in order to meet your annual sales targets for any given territory, market or product. (We shall look later at how sales forces might be organised, whether by region, product, market, or even customer size.) Next, estimate the total number of calls required to bring in the sales you seek from these prospects. Remember that these calls need to reflect the differing needs of maintaining and increasing *existing* business (existing customers are always easier to keep than capturing new ones), as well as the winning of *new* business. Accordingly, ask each member of the team to grade their customers and targeted prospects by the number of visits they believe are required over the year. You might, as a simple example, decide to grade your customers and prospects into five categories, some of which may need to be called upon twice a month and others only twice a year. The analysis might then look like this:

Example: Customer Categorisation

Category A	5 prospects require 24 visits/year =	120 visits
Category B	30 prospects require 12 visits/year =	360 visits
Category C	115 prospects require 6 visits/year =	690 visits
Category D	180 prospects require 4 visits/year =	720 visits

Category E 420 prospects require 2 visits/year = 840 visits

Thus 750 prospects require a total of 3060 visits

Add say 10% for misc. calls = 306 visits

Therefore TOTAL VISITS NEEDED = 3366 visits.

Note the distribution of customers indicated above, which is quite realistic. The top three categories account for only 20 per cent of the customer and prospect base, but take up nearly 40 per cent of all the sales calls planned. If your business follows the Pareto principle (the top 20 per cent of customers account for 80 per cent of the business), this loading of calls in favour of those customers requiring the most frequent calls (because presumably, they have the largest sales potential) is not at all unreasonable. Just to check this, you might then calculate the sales volume which you target from each of these top three categories, to ensure that it does account for about the same percentage of sales calls – i.e. 40 per cent in the case above. If not, you may well wish to query and review your sales team's judgement on their allocation of calling priorities.)

Now, work out how many sales days there are in a year. Assuming 46 working weeks, less perhaps 2 weeks each year for training and sales meetings and say ½ a day a week for planning and reporting, that is $44 \times 4\frac{1}{2} = 198$ selling days per full-time sales person per year.

In our example, there are 3366 total visits required. Dividing this number by 198 days/person/year indicates that 17 calls have to be made, on average, each sales day. That leaves you now to set a target for how many visits you can realistically expect your team to make each selling day. If your business can expect 8 calls a day from each person, you could say that you only need 2 sales people if you can persuade them to increase that target to 8½ calls each. For a small regional business with calls close together, that may be achievable. Alternatively, you might say that 4½ calls is more realistic for a nationwide business, in which case you need a sales team of 4 (4 × 4½ = 18 calls a day, leaving one call/day safety margin).

76

More practically, you might feel that two sales people in regions which are more densely packed with customers may make, say, 5 calls a day, but elsewhere only 4 calls can be achieved on average, which would still suggest you need a sales team of 4 (2 × 5 calls/day and 2 × 4 = 4 sales people), but with different work-loads.

Sales revenue per sales person

The sort of analysis given in the above example is a good start. It ensures that customers are divided into categories of importance and it also demands the setting of call-rate targets. There are two major shortcomings.

The first consideration that is missing from the above is a calculation of the sales volume generated by sales person, and the resulting profitability. Research in the UK in 1988 by *Sales Direction Magazine* shows a very broad spread of sales per sales person in practice, from under £100,000 (14 per cent of those surveyed) to over £2 million (15 per cent). Twenty per cent of all companies surveyed occupied the most common band of £250,000 to £500,000 sales per sales person.

Now, suppose in our worked example of customer categorisation that the *total* sales revenue of the company is only £500,000; then a sales team of four people will generate but a modest £125,000 each on average. If you calculate that each sales person, complete with company car, expenses, national insurance costs and so on, costs £30,000 (not an unreasonable figure at the time of writing), this is 24 per cent of the total sales revenue produced:

$$\left(\pounds\, \frac{30,000}{125,000} \times 100 \right) = 24\%$$

Can your business afford this? If not, you had better see how you can make more calls in a day, increase the sales revenue per customer, or even consider making fewer calls per customer. (We look at monitoring these target ratios in the next section.)

Variations in sales load

The second consideration is equally practical. Not all businesses are quite so simple. For businesses which require a large degree of new sales prospecting, for example, order patterns may be much less predictable. The sales value of each enquiry or order may vary significantly, as may the conversion rate of enquiries to orders. The number of visits that are targeted for selling, as opposed to those aimed at servicing customers, collecting bad debts or researching market information, may also vary significantly. Key customers who are large will need regular visits to ensure maintenance of their business; key prospects will also need regular visits, but of a different sort. If you don't set targets for these too, your sales team may well make the requisite number of calls but you could still miss your overall sales target by a long way.

A solution to this is to analyse the work-load further by applying an analysis which we might rather grandiosely entitle 'Thorn's Formula for Sales Optimisation'. It may appear at first sight to be a highly theoretical approach. However, when applied intelligently and not unduly mechanistically, it can provide a very useful 'what if?' model for optimising your sales returns.

Sales optimisation

First, there are some sales variables to identify, which you can measure and then track. They might be as follows:

Let your sales or orders target be $= £$

Total orders expected in the year be $= 0$

(Thus your average order value is $= \frac{£}{0}$)

Let the number of quotes/year be $= Q$

sales visits/year	= **Vsales** or **Vs**
total visits/year	= **Vtotal** or **Vt**
total sales days	= **Dsales** or **Ds**
total working days	= **Dtotal** or **Dt**.

Then, if only by simple mathematical inspection, you can see that the orders you need to generate each day (**£/Dt**) are a function of:

$$\frac{£}{Dt} = \frac{£}{0} \times \frac{0}{Q} \times \frac{Q}{Vs} \times \frac{Vs}{Vt} \times \frac{Vt}{Ds} \times \frac{Ds}{Dt}$$

or, in plain English,

Orders per day = *average order value* $(\frac{£}{0})$,

times the average *conversion rate* of enquiries to orders $(\frac{0}{Q})$,

times the average number of enquiries received per sales call, or *quotation efficiency* $(\frac{Q}{Vs})$,

times the *sales visit rate*, or proportion of sales visits to total visits $(\frac{Vs}{Vt})$,

times the number of calls made per selling day $(\frac{Vt}{Ds})$,

times the *available sales days ratio*, expressed as a proportion of the total working days $(\frac{Ds}{Dt})$.

(Note, for the sake of simplicity, the assumption that orders received in the period in question will equal sales made. You may find the former easier to measure than the latter.)

We will look at some of these variables in the next section under *Reporting* and *Controls*, because they are clearly targets that need to be monitored. Figure 11 in that section will suggest how. At this stage, however, we are still in the planning phase. It is important to establish what these ratios currently are for your business, if you do not already know. Now set new targets which you believe could be achieved by attention to each of these key ratios.

You will soon see that quite modest improvements can make significant changes to the number of sales days (and therefore sales people) you need. Alternatively, and more positively, the extra sales days created by improving efficiency can be used to bring in yet more business.

From here, it is but a short step to tailoring this formula to include other parameters particularly relevant to your business. For example, you may be interested in monitoring not just sales revenue but also unit price and volume. If so, you can break down the $\frac{£}{Dt}$ ratio as follows:

$$\textbf{Orders per day} = \frac{£}{Dt} = \textbf{Unit price}\left(\frac{£}{\textbf{unit}}\right) \times \textbf{Units ordered}$$

$$\textbf{per day}\left(\frac{\textbf{Units}}{\textbf{Dt}}\right).$$

You may also want to consider the credit control aspect. After all, goods or services invoiced only represent money in the bank when the invoices have been paid in full. (Note also that you will probably only want to pay sales commission on money received, not invoiced.) Accordingly, you might monitor goods invoiced (£i) *and* moneys paid (£p). $\frac{£p}{£i}$ then becomes an important *credit control ratio* which should be as close to 1 as possible. Your business may also be highly dependent upon having your goods or services demonstrated by your sales team, so you may need to monitor the *quotations to demonstrations ratio* $\left(\frac{Q}{Dem}\right)$. Further, you may wish to monitor *demonstrations/enquiries ratios* $\left(\dfrac{\mathbf{Dem}}{\mathbf{E}}\right)$ to complete the selling sequence.

A more complete version of the equation might therefore read:

Sales income received (i.e. paid) **per day** $=$

$$\frac{\pounds p}{Dt} = \frac{\pounds p}{Unit} \times \frac{Units}{Dt}$$

$$= \frac{\pounds p}{\pounds i}\ (credit\ ratio) \times \frac{\pounds i}{O}\ (average\ order\ value) \times \frac{O}{Q}\ (conversion$$

$$rate) \times \frac{Q}{Dem}(demo\ success\ rate) \times \frac{Dem}{E}\ (enquiry\ interest$$

$$factor) \times \frac{E}{Vs}(enquiry\ per\ visit\ ratio) \times \frac{Vs}{Vt}\ (sales\ visit\ rate)$$

$$\times \frac{Vt}{Ds}\ (calls\ per\ day) \times \frac{Ds}{Dt}\ (available\ sales\ days\ ratio).$$

(Note once again that orders received are assumed, for simplicity, to equal sales invoiced.)

Other ratios that can be monitored in the same way are miles driven per day or per call, cost per sales visit, the ratio of after-sales or prospecting calls to total calls, and so on. These can be covered by the same overall approach if such differentiation is relevant to your market-place.

A benefit of this rigorously analytical procedure, apart from optimising your sales efficiency by breaking down your targets into smaller, easily identifiable items, is that you can apply the formula to a complete sales team, or just a region, or even one individual or product. For example, a classic complaint from sales people is that pre-ordained call rates take no account of the extended visit to a large site with many sub-buying units, or the call to negotiate a particularly large contract: these might result in a call rate that plummets to perhaps only one call a day on occasions. The classic response is that these targets are only averages and that meeting the final sales target is, overall, the more important requirement. However, by using this formula to take account of the specific needs of one person's territory, you can set targets that do reflect individual circumstances.

Key accounts

Your business may be particularly dependent upon a few key customers. These will need a very specific and tailored sales plan and strategy to maximise the advantage that such companies can offer a supplier. The approach described above can be especially powerful.

First, set up a key-account team just for these customers. Staff this team with your best sales people who know your product range particularly well, and who have also been specially trained in large-contract negotiating.

Now set target ratios for call rate, order value and so on, which are specifically designed to meet the needs of this premium business. By isolating these targets from those for the rest of your business, you now acquire an additional benefit. You can give the results of this team of sharpshooters the special management attention they deserve, both in reviewing progress and in taking pre-emptive sales action as circumstances demand.

This can include focusing on special pricing strategies, such as annual contracts or volume-rebate schemes, organising special delivery options, own-branding and so on. Special attention to key accounts also arms you better to fight competitors, who will also be attracted by the rich pickings that larger customers can provide. Such an approach also serves to highlight to your team the importance and influence of larger users, in terms of your company's profitability and market share.

Cold calling/prospecting

Prospecting for new business needs special attention. You may well feel that it is worth creating special targets for this important activity. Cold calling, or prospecting for new business without prior appointment, needs a careful balance of judgement. If too little time is spent calling this way, it is probable that your sales team are not making the fullest use of their time. For example, there will always be occasions when a journey plan finishes earlier than expected, which should allow time for chance leads to be followed up or exploratory calls to be made to unknown and nearby companies. If they do not exploit such opportunities, your team may not be planting adequate seed-corn for growing an expanded customer base for the future. Your sales team can't expect *all* your new customers to come from respondents to your brilliant promotional work; you may well feel that some new prospects should be generated by the sales team's own exploratory efforts.

On the other hand, you don't want your team making too many cold calls, unannounced and unplanned. Such calls can be very inefficient ways to gather essential customer knowledge, and will probably have a high failure rate. Often the people called on won't be realistic prospects anyway, or the right person may not be available. In any event, there is a strong sales maxim, which we shall refer to again under *Promotion* in the 'Marketing' section, that you should never sell to strangers. Ideally, new prospects should already know your company and its products – at least by repute.

Accordingly, the balance of sales effort in most companies will probably be against making too many cold calls. After all, it is generally much easier to win additional business from existing accounts rather than from new ones. Prospecting takes a lot of digging and generally consumes much more time than repeat calls. However, against that, it must be said that the joy and reward of making a *successful* cold call, perhaps helped by being at the right place just at the right time, takes a lot of beating. Many would say that the skill of making successful cold calls requires the highest order of sales skills, and indeed some businesses have a tradition of relying heavily on this method of acquiring new customers.

We shall look at keeping a record of potential new customers – the 'Prospect Bank' – in the next section on 'Reporting and Controls'.

Call-planning

Planning a visit programme carefully is an essential skill for any professional sales force. Time spent travelling is time lost for selling. Left to the whims of individual sales people, journey plans can represent the tracks of a demented dog in search of stray rabbits and other interesting diversions, rather than a well-thought-out plan co-ordinated by a professional manager. Your sales team costs far too much to allow this to happen and it is your job, as sales manager, to control this.

For businesses with many repeat sales, route-planning may be much easier than for companies in the capital goods sector, for example, where any planning must in the end be subservient to the timing of the demands and opportunities of the market-place. However, where there is a pattern of needs for sales visits, calls and journey routes should be planned.

Useful Exercise: Journey-planning

For each member of the team, you need to plot on a large road map where each customer and major prospect lies. Having divided these companies up into categories of frequency of visit needed, the task is to find the optimum route which will cover the territory in the least time. After all, some research shows that many sales teams actually spend less than one hour a day in front of prospects who have authority (and the need) to buy. Unbelievable? – then check with your own team! You may be unpleasantly surprised.

After the calls have been plotted on a map, one option is to subdivide the territory into smaller segments, so that each segment is visited every fourth week for example. Alternatively, if this is not possible or realistic, identify each customer who must be called upon in a given time and place a pin in the map. Now take a piece of cotton and track what you feel is the best route. Note that the shortest route will usually be the one that crosses over itself or overlaps the least. Having measured the overall distance, try alternative routes. When you have found the shortest one possible, try it out yourself to see if a slightly longer route – on a motorway, for example – might be quicker.

If you have any doubt as to whether a shorter distance or a shorter time is more important, cost it. Extra miles can be costed at the rate for the size of vehicle (£0.35/mile, for example). If the cost of a sales person is £30,000 p.a., working perhaps 198 sales days a year, with say 7½ selling hours available a day, that cost is £0.34 per selling minute. These figures may only be approximate, but they show that each mile saved by a 'short cut' is only valuable if it takes less than 62 seconds more than a longer but speedier route, assuming of course that those seconds are genuinely useful. You could easily lose that time by going directly through a busy town, rather than using the bypass.

When you have completed your analysis, you may well find that the real problem is that your sales representative is living in the wrong place, or is not prepared to stay away from home. Both of these issues need to be addressed if you are going to have a successful organisation.

Sales organisation

These considerations may well also lead you to question how best to deploy your sales team. You have a number of options. In the survey by Industrial Market Research Ltd of over 300 companies in the UK, organisation by sales area was, not surprisingly, the most popular and accounted for 81 per cent of all companies contacted. However, the survey also showed other methods of organising sales resources. These included division by product type (18 per cent), end-user industry (17 per cent) and size of customer (9 per cent). In fact 24 per cent of companies favoured using *several* methods of organising their troops – especially the larger ones employing over 1,000, of which as many as 42 per cent reported using several different methods of allocating sales responsibilities.

There is no doubt that the whole question of sales organisation tends to suffer from cyclical changes of fashion, especially in larger companies. Perhaps you have seen something like the following little cameo before.

'You may well find that the real problem is that your sales representative is living in the wrong place.'

The sales team of Ye Olde Widget Company Ltd was organised by geographic responsibility because this was seen to be the most cost-effective method. Anyway, that was how it had always been done. In due course, the owner handed over to a new boss, who immediately hired a consultant to review the business. After some study, it was suggested that greater product specialisation was necessary. The market-place was becoming increasingly complex and fragmented. Accordingly, the company was split into a number of specialist product divisions, each with its own sales team.

Product specialisation worked most satisfactorily for some years. However, those larger customers who bought from more than one division began to complain. They were receiving visits from several different divisions of Ye Olde Widget Company Ltd, who by the way were now called Hi-Tech Widgets plc, causing all sorts of confusion. Buyers would sometimes receive two or three salesmen a day from the same company, and were never quite sure who could take responsibility for what. After some soul-searching at Hi-Tech Widgets a grand new plan was implemented and product divisions were abandoned. This was acclerated, some cynics said, by complaints from Accounts that, since each division sent their own separate invoices to the same customers, debt-collection had become a nightmare. The new plan that was announced meant a further change in the organisation of the sales team; this time market focus would be the goal. Instead of organising sales teams by product specialisation they would all become market specialists and any given customer would receive visits from only one salesman.

That was a great idea, everyone agreed, and it worked rather well. There was no customer overlap and Accounts were delighted. In due course, however, just after they were taken over, as a matter of fact, and renamed Trans-World (Widgets) Inc., further complaints surfaced, this time from the new owners. They complained that new and growing sectors of the market-place were not being covered properly. Further, some product lines were being undersold because the sales team, who after all had been product specialists until recently, knew some products very well but others not at all. The sales director also noticed that, since the abandonment of geographic specialisation, selling costs had rocketed because most sales teams had to cover the full length and breadth of the country in order to reach all the customers in their given market sector.

Then entered an even wiser (and more expensive) consultant. He determined that what was required was a matrix organisation. 'We should have sales teams divided by geographic responsibilities,' he declared, 'and supported by product managers. Their job will be to assist the geographic sales teams with their special product-expertise and marketing skills.' That was marvellous – the best of all worlds. Some had heard about matrix management, but to most it was new, and vibrant, and exciting. It was also rather costly.

It was when they changed their name to TW Inc. that one of the Twinklies (as the wags in the sales teams had learned to style themselves) noted that any given customer now received visits not just from a regional salesman, but also from several product specialists, who were still being torn into pieces by having to cover the whole country. Worse, there were now both sales and product managers fighting each other over sales policy. Confusion reigned supreme.

Like all good stories, however, this has a happy ending. All it took was the next downturn in the market and near-bankruptcy. A happy story, you ask? Of course! The company was sold back to the original owner.

His first task was to revive past glories and change the name – to Ye Olde International Widget Company (1990) Ltd. Then the new finance director had a brain-wave. 'Look how much money we can save if we get rid of all our product specialists!' he exclaimed. 'They were becoming unwieldy prima donnas anyway,' muttered a regional sales manager sourly. Immediately, the sales teams converted back to their original, straightforward geographic split. Everyone was now back where they started.

The only thing that had really changed in the meantime was their long-suffering customers. Most of them had moved their business to a mail-order house long ago. But that's another story.

This tale may seem rather cynical but, amusement apart, it reflects many companies' problems. The difficulty is that in many such organisations there is *no* correct solution to how a sales team should be organised. The real lesson is to operate with the smallest possible resources, commensurate with providing the maximum market coverage most cost-effectively, and apply these resources intelligently. Be flexible, and don't feel that what you do in the South-East for example has to be the same in the North-West. If one person covers a bigger area, or product range or market spread, so be it.

Sales channel

Of course you don't have to sell through a field-sales team, anyway; you can also sell through agents and distributors, by direct mail and telesales, by 'party-plan', by franchising and so on. We look at some of these options in the 'Marketing' section later, under *Placement/Distribution*. Naturally, your choice will significantly affect the sales resources you need, and how they are to be organised.

Further, not all companies will sell direct to end-users. This option may be the most attractive to a prime supplier or manufacturer, especially in highly competitive markets where there may be little room for other companies in the distribution chain to add their profit margin as well. However, some markets will be too diffuse to allow this – and others will be protected by historical trading links which favour the regional middle-man or specialist distributor, for example. Some market channels can be quite complex, where the product is sold through wholesalers, trade dealers, both, or even direct to end-users but via one or more nominated wholesalers and dealers. If there is a strong tradition of using one particular distribution route in your market, there may be rich prizes to be won by adopting a radical departure from the norm. However, the risks can be high. Be counselled therefore that it is unwise to break new ground this way, without researching buying habits and customer attitudes very carefully.

One example of such a break with tradition can be those companies who supply original equipment manufacturers (OEMs). It may be very attractive for such companies to consider bypassing the OEM, in order to sell direct to the OEM's end-users and after-market. You have a choice, but your decision will have to balance the greater profit potential for yourself against the power and influence an OEM can exercise in a market through control of specifications, design, and even guarantees of their equipment. This can be an exciting route to take, but be forewarned that you will probably find that you cannot supply both sectors, for then you will be competing with your own customers.

Useful Exercise: Channel-mapping

Take a look at how your business goes to market, and compare it with your competitors'. Divide each stage of the distribution route of all suppliers into distinct categories, from the manufacturer to distributors, wholesalers and other middle-men, OEMs and other specifiers (who may be architects, local government or large contractors), and on to the eventual end-users. Quite probably there will be several branches containing several different routes.

Now try and break down the total value of the market through each branch of the route, back to each of the major suppliers. You may well note that those supplying imported goods, for example, go through quite different routes, as may the really large and the much smaller producers. Where do you fit in? Could you make savings by eliminating a step in the chain? Could you take additional market share by adding new distribution routes to your customer base? Look out for any areas of potential conflict, and decide where the greater benefits might come from. Cost out the extra expense – and savings – that may be involved, and then consider what special skills and strengths your sales force will need to take the fullest advantage of new routes.

If you spot new opportunities, discuss these widely with your team and your senior colleagues before you act. If there are any doubts, consider investing in more market research. Market intelligence and understanding is a vital requirement for any strategic change. Then, before you proceed, ensure that all the key players, including your sales team, your major customers and even your new prospects, are appropriately and fully briefed. You want your competitors to be surprised – not your own side.

10 Reporting, Controls and Leadership

'We do not learn to know men through their coming to us. To find what sort of persons they are, we must go to them.'

J. W. von Goethe

Having planned the organisation of your troops, it is now necessary to make sure that your plans happen, and to take corrective action where necessary. To do this, you need to know what is going on in your market-place, in detail. This is where the key ratios we discussed in the preceding chapter come in to play.

Key ratios

Daily sales (or order) rate (£p/Dt). This is probably the eventual sales target, accumulated over the year perhaps, by which you will be judged. If your business is seasonal, you will need to flex this target accordingly.

In turn, this target is a product of average unit sales price $\left(\dfrac{£p}{Unit}\right)$ and daily sales or order volume $\left(\dfrac{Units}{Dt}\right)$. You might meet your overall target, but still find the business is in trouble because these subsidiary factors are not as you planned. The first, average units sales price, will give a useful guide to the sales mix. A figure lower than targeted will indicate that the sales mix of the overall sales figure is slanted towards the lower end of the price range. This may have quite important repercussions on profitability, if your higher-priced products tend to have the better margins. The second ratio, unit sales or orders per day, may show up particularly important capacity considerations. Too high a figure, and you may not be able to meet demand. Too low and you may have to reinvigorate your sales efforts or consider revising your sales forecast.

All other subdivisions of these ratios, covered in the last section, add further insight into whether your daily sales rate is on track or not. You should aim to have control of all of them. Recalling that the full equation was:

Sales income received (i.e. paid) **per day** =

$$\frac{£p}{Dt} = \frac{£p}{Unit} \times \frac{Units}{Dt}$$

$$= \frac{£p}{£i} \ (credit\ ratio) \times \frac{£i}{0} \ (average\ order\ value) \times \frac{O}{Q} \ (conversion$$

$$rate) \times \frac{Q}{Dem}(demo\ success\ rate) \times \frac{Dem}{E} \ (enquiry\ interest$$

$$factor) \times \frac{E}{Vs}(enquiry\ per\ visit\ ratio) \times \frac{Vs}{Vt} \ (sales\ visit\ rate)$$

$$\times \frac{Vt}{Ds} \ (calls\ per\ day) \times \frac{Ds}{Dt} \ (available\ sales\ days\ ratio).$$

some of the key ratios, against which you need to set targets and monitor actual performance, include:

Credit ratio (£p/£i)

Almost any business will have to plan for some bad debts, unless it can trade strictly on cash-in-advance terms (could yours?). The sales team has a very important role to play here, which is why sales bonuses should only be paid against moneys received rather than sales invoiced. The sales team should be encouraged to play a part in credit-risk assessments and in deciding what terms of payment may be allowed. If necessary, they should also be encouraged to help in debt collection. Ideally, sales teams should not have to collect debts, but sometimes their inside knowledge will be vital.

Average order value ($£i/0$)

Some orders are too small to be worth chasing, unless you can charge a suitable small-order premium, or minimum order charge. Naturally, you would like your average order value to be as high as possible. You can influence this both by strategic pricing policy and tactical sales instruction.

Conversion rate ($0/Q$)

The conversion rate of quotations to orders, also known as *strike rate*, is a function of two things under your control. The first is the ability of your sales team, and the conversion rate will provide a useful indicator of individuals' training needs. The second is the company's ability to generate meaningful and relevant enquiries in the first place. This in turn can be monitored by choosing your own ratios, such as *quotations to enquiries, demonstrations to enquiries, enquiries to sales visits*, etc. We shall look at the whole aspect of obtaining and qualifying leads in the 'Marketing' section, later on.

Sales visit rate (Vs/Vt) *and available sales days* (Ds/Dt)

Some sales teams are structured only to follow up leads and follow them through until they become orders. The rest is left to other specialist functions. In other companies, the sales force is expected to provide its own leads and prospects, to provide technical back-up and after-sales service, all without additional assistance. Equally, some sales forces are expected to do their planning and reporting outside office hours, with hardly any time off the road for training, sales meetings and accompanied works visits by customers, while others may only spend part of their time in front of their customers. Whatever your circumstances, you are unlikely to meet your sales targets if your sales visit rate and available sales days ratios are not also on target.

Calls per day (**Vt/Ds**)

Raising this target as high as possible is superficially one of the easiest ways to increase sales performance, but it needs careful handling. It is not just a matter of recognising that some calls will take much longer than others, as already mentioned. If you place too much emphasis on call rates, it is the easiest thing in the world for 'ghost' visits to be added to the call sheet, to make the rate look better than it really is. Sometimes, you may feel it is necessary to ring up a small sample of customers just to check that visits claimed have genuinely been made, but such an action has to herald the beginning of the end for the sales person in question. It is much better in the first place to breed that sense of trust and responsibility which is essential for all members of staff, but especially those who spend the majority of their time unsupervised off-site.

Targets

With all these ratios, it is important to keep an eye on the essentials, and make sure that the targets which are fundamental to success are fully communicated to, and understood by, your team. Slavish or mechanistic adherence to detailed targets may be just as unproductive as having none at all. It is also clearly important to keep an eye on circumstances as they change.

In order to monitor your actual performance against your targets, you should keep a regular record in a format such as indicated in Figure 11. The order and quotation data should come from your sales office, and the details on the number of sales visits made and the number of working days allocated to selling (as opposed to training, sales meetings, etc.) should come from your sales team's call reports, which we will look at under *Reporting systems*.

Figure 11: Sales Performance Record

REGION: _____ REP.: _____ DATE: _____

DATA		TARGET		ACTUAL	
		PERIOD	YEAR TO DATE	PERIOD	YEAR TO DATE
Order value	£				
No. of orders	O				
No. of quotes	Q				
Sales visits	Vs				
Total visits	Vt				
Sales days	Ds				
Total days	Dt				
Orders/Day	£/Dt				
Average order value	£/O				
Quote efficiency	Q/Vs				
Visit ratio	Vs/Vt				
Call rate	Vt/Ds				
Sales days	Ds/Dt				

Note that the sales performance record can be built up from individual records to produce an overall figure for the company. Naturally this is a vital tool for **forecasting** which we shall also look at later. If your targets do not reflect the reality of your market-place, you may fool yourself, but you will not fool your team. The outcome of this can only be a demotivated sales force that does not respect you, failed sales targets and a slow exodus to pastures new, with the better sales people leading the way.

Consequently, in order to keep in touch with market conditions, you need:

- to make regular visits to customers with each of your sales team in turn,

- a regular review of performance, and

95

- good reporting procedures that reflect the needs of your business.

Leadership

Whether in matters of policy, setting broad targets and objectives, or more detailed direction, leadership is of course a matter of personal style. You do need to project yourself, but project yourself as you are rather than as you would like your team to see you. Any pretence will be seen through and you won't be respected for it. If you are not a 'Gung-ho chaps, over the wall and at 'em!' type, don't try to be. Strong leadership styles come in many guises, but the essentials should always include:

- a strong sense of vision and clearly communicated direction;

- a firm insistence that once decisions are made, they are executed;

- reward for good results and insistence that poor results are improved upon, with provision of the right tools to succeed;

- the allocation of tasks, rewards and rebukes, fairly and without favour.

To this list of essentials, most would recommend adding the involvement of your team in decision-making. This does *not* mean taking a democratic vote, because decisions for which you are responsible must stay your responsibility. It does mean, however, listening to the advice, recommendations and comments of your team and respecting their judgement. If you don't agree with what you are being told, then have no hesitation in saying so, but listen carefully first. A good leader is never above taking counsel, if it is wise, from any source, especially from within his or her own team.

'Accompanied visits present an ideal opportunity to identify training needs and offer encouragement.'

Accompanied visits

Leadership *in the field* is another important part of a manager's job. Accompanied visits not only allow you to keep in touch with your sales team and the market-place, they also present an ideal opportunity to identify training needs and offer encouragement. Note that these visits are *not* to give your sales team a rest while you do all the work. That is not leadership. Your job is to observe and support when needed.

To make the best of these visits, try to draw up your own check-list of points to monitor, and keep a record for subsequent occasions. At the end of each accompanied visit make time to sit down and review the outcome, comparing progress made against previous accompanied calls. You will have your own ideas about what you are looking for, but each phase of the sales visit, from the opening through to proposing and closing, should be monitored. The check-list in Figure 12 may help you.

Figure 12: Check-list for Accompanied Visit

Date: _____ Sales representative: _____

Customer: _____ Location: _____

Contact(s): _____

Advance planning

- Advance knowledge of the account/prospect?

- The reason for calling?

- Are the objectives realistic, and ambitious enough?

- How are these objectives to be achieved?

- Was an appointment made? (If not, why not?)

98

The approach

- Quality of relationship established?

- Were the decision-makers and influencers properly identified?

- Quality of questions asked?

- Were the answers listened to intelligently?

- How well were the customer's needs established?

The sale

- How closely were these needs linked to the benefits offered by your products or services?

- How well was your company presented?

- How well were the products/services presented?

- Were these presentations relevant?

- Were sales aids used with maximum effect?

- Were the sales aids in good condition?

- How well were objections handled?

- Were buying signals recognised?

- Was the appropriate style and timing of closing used?

- Were opportunities to sell add-on products taken?

- Were comprehensive notes taken?

- Is it clear who has to do what, next?

- Were referrals for use elsewhere solicited?

Leaving

- How was the finish of the call handled?

- Have the visit report and any action lists been filled in properly?

- What follow-up system is used for the next time?

General

- Personal presentation and dress?

- Overall product knowledge?

- Sales skills?

- Mental attitude?

- Other comments?

- Items handled particularly well.

- Areas for improvement and suggestions for next time.

- Training needs.

Appraisals

Appraising members of a sales team requires tact and diplomacy, especially at the end of an accompanied visit which may well have presented its own special problems and pressures for your colleague. Your visits will count for much in your team's mind and you need to make the most of them. They will rightly look to you for guidance and inspiration, so your comments need to be positive, objective and fair. Remember that no one likes criticism unless it is felt that it is designed to help and is not offered in a spirit of animosity. Ensure that your comments therefore give some personal benefit to your colleague, and are not an excuse for you to release pent-up emotion.

If you have a negative comment to make, you should not hold back from making it, but praise the good aspects first. Then ask your colleague to offer his or her own personal appraisal before wading in. Try to avoid making your comments too personal. You can do this by asking open-ended questions. For example: 'Do you think XYZ was a buying signal?', rather than 'You weren't concentrating. You missed that comment about XYZ altogether, didn't you?' Ask what your colleague felt pleased about and what was particularly good. You can lead into the less positive aspects by your colleague's omissions, using the check-list in Figure 12 to help you.

Beyond these accompanied visits, you should also appraise your colleagues more formally, on a regular basis, away from the pressures and interruptions of a busy sales day. Use the information and impressions you have gained from your accompanied visits to help you, but take the opportunity to discuss the broader issues of interest to you, and to your colleagues, as well.

As with your accompanied visits, you should draw up your own check-list. There is no reason why you should not give this to your team in advance and ask them to score themselves. Self-analysis is often more valuable than any other. Items for discussion should include those indicated in Figure 13.

Figure 13: Check-list for Formal Appraisals

- A review of targets against actual sales performance.

- A review of future targets and how these are to be accomplished.

- General sales skills, product and market knowledge.

- Awareness of company strategy related to the market-place and competitor activity, etc;

- Personal attitude, work ethic and relations with colleagues;

- Personal appearance and discipline, time-keeping, adherence to company policies, the upkeep of records, maintenance of sales aids and the company car, etc;

- Promotion ambitions and prospects;

- Training needs and areas for improvement.

- An agreed summary of all the above.

Before you finish any appraisal, make sure that you have obtained agreement on the key issues arising and agree when the next review will take place. Never voice comparisons with other members of your team. Your specific comments or advice should be for the individual's ears and not for general publication.

Discipline

It is worth mentioning here the subject of discipline in its own right. Sales people are generally independent types. They need to be. But managing independent souls who see their managers only on occasions can be difficult. You must give your team room to take personal initiatives or you will have a sales team that may do nothing wrong, but nothing special either.

The skill is to set essential standards, rules and regulations, which *must* be met by everyone. These need to be as few as possible, compatible with your company's own style and procedures, but non-negotiable. Waver on these and effectively you have no standards. Everyone will then do what *they* think is right, or convenient.

When these requirements are not met, you must act firmly. A breach of discipline is effectively a breach of trust and it is important your staff see things this way too. Dependent upon the severity of any failing, you must issue a verbal warning, confirmed in writing, stating the consequences of any repetition of the offence. If the breach is sufficiently serious, you must be prepared even to make a dismissal. Allow as much time as it takes to hear all sides of the argument, and retrain if you have to, but don't let personal feelings of pity or friendship sway your judgement. You have a responsibility for what is a very costly operation, and you do not discharge that responsibility if you allow malpractice to persist.

Reporting systems

These will be the mainstay, for most companies, in controlling resources and keeping regularly in touch with the market-place. Few teams will not have some of the following list of systems, but few will have them all. Before you implement a new system, make sure that the potential benefits will indeed be realised. Before you dispense with one, just check that you really can do without it.

Journey plans

These have two main functions. The first is to ensure that routes are given the planning and thought they deserve. There is no reason why urgent and unplanned calls should not be added as necessary, but an unplanned day (or week) is likely to be a wasted one. The other purpose is to let you and other colleagues back at base know where each member of the team is, in case urgent contact is necessary.

Most companies find that a weekly plan, filed by the Monday morning of that week, is quite adequate. For each day, morning and afternoon, you need to know the name and location of each call, the name and job title of the principal contact or contacts, and a brief description of the objective of each call.

Call reports

These may well vary in length in inverse proportion to the number of calls made each day. The greater the number of calls, the shorter will probably be the report.

Several proprietary systems are available for recording and analysing this information, some of which are designed to incorporate the information already entered on the journey plans the previous week. The essential feature of any system is that it should be quick and easy to use, without dispensing with key information. A neat way of handling this is to have a printed form which just requires ticks in boxes for basic information, with just a small space for other details.

You may prefer to design your own call report sheet. If so, think carefully about what information you really need, and what you will do with it.

For example, do you wish to distinguish between:

● cold calls and those where appointments have been made;

● calls designed to pick up enquiries, those designed to convert quotations into sales, after-sales calls, and those made for market intelligence purposes?

Do you need to register:

● aborted calls (contact not available), or

● telephone calls?

Presumably you will certainly wish to include:

● the contacts, the company and its location,

● the main objectives and reason for calling,

● the key products, services or market intelligence discussed,

● the outcome (enquiry, product demonstration, order, complaint, chance to rebid or whatever), and

● the follow-up action, which should include the planned date for the next visit.

Some managers may wish to monitor the exact times of arrival and departure, plus the miles travelled from the previous call. This information can be very useful as an additional control, but it all takes time to log, and even more time to note back at the office.

Call reports should be completed at the end of each visit (or at the very least, at the end of each day, without fail), and should be returned to you at least weekly. Don't forget to note the data relevant for the sales performance record, such as described in Figure 11 earlier.

It makes good sense to check that the visits made each day bear some resemblance to the journey plan submitted in advance. It is also very important that any particular points arising should be commented upon as soon as possible. These may be matters of discipline ('Why only two calls on Wednesday afternoon?' 'Why didn't you call in to see ABC on the way to XYZ?' etc.) or business ('Try and find out more about our competitor's reasons for withdrawing LMN.' 'Don't offer the 123 model for that application, it won't work. They need the 123X.').

Action sheets

If there is anything major to report, it should go on a separate sheet in more detail, along with any specific request for action. These action sheets (one for each event) should be guaranteed top priority back at base, and should be sent to you daily. If the action requested has been the subject of a telephone call the same day, a confirming action sheet should still be written, but marked 'Confirmation only; refer to telecon on XYZ with ABC.'

Customer records

These invariably present a problem. You want a master copy for the sales office, and your people in the field need a copy too. If the sales office has a copy, can you be sure the records will be updated? If the sales force have copies, can you be sure you can recover them if someone leaves? (The answer to the last point must be 'Yes', however you choose to administrate this. All records, like the company car, must be returned intact when someone leaves.)

Deciding who should have copies of customer records will be governed by the need. You may well feel that the sales-office copy only requires administrative information to be noted, such as principal contacts (with full job title, initials and names spelt correctly), trading terms and addresses for routine mail, invoices and deliveries. This information should go on the computer if you have one (which should also tell you the trading history), so you can run mail shots etc. Make sure that the sales person in charge of the account *and* someone in the office have joint responsibility for keeping the files updated (through the action-sheet system, if you like).

You may well feel that the sales teams' customer record system needs to be rather different. Good practice is to include travel directions (for someone new, one day, if for no one else); all the contacts, their names, job titles and real levels of responsibility; products of relevance to that account and likely consumption, together with your and any competitors' share of that consumption; a record of previous visits and their outcome, plus any correspondence; and any other key information – contacts' personal interests and pet hates, the earliest and latest time to call, and so on. Smart sales people will also record the names of key contacts' secretaries, the telephonist, and anyone else who can achieve access where they themselves might not otherwise.

Many companies, including yours, will probably already employ most if not all of the above records. What about some of these below, which will be found less frequently?

Prospect bank

This is a simple record of companies in the territory who are not yet regular customers. Some will already have had calls, others may be new. These are the seed-corn for future growth. You may well wish to set a target for how many are visited in any given period. The record should contain all the basic details as in a customer record, as and when they become available, but should be kept separately to highlight the different style of approach that may well be necessary. See Figure 14 for an example.

Figure 14: Prospect Bank

REGION: _____ REPRESENTATIVE _____

NAME	POTENTIAL AND PRESENT SUPPLIERS: ....
....	....
ADDRESS:	....
....	....
....	....
PHONE NO	....
CONTACT	....

PROBLEMS	ADDITIONAL COMMENTS

DATE OF CALL	OUTCOME OF CALL	
....	....	
....	....	
....	....	
....	....	
....	....	

VISIT ANALYSIS	DATE	NOTES
INITIAL VISIT	....	
RECALL	....	
SURVEY	....	
QUOTE	....	
REVIEW 1, 2, 3	....	
CLOSE/CONVERSION	....	
CUSTOMER FILE STARTED	....	
REVIEW	....	

Prospect planner

Each quarter, say, each salesman or woman should log the companies to whom sales calls will be made. Against each customer or prospect, the planner should indicate the volume of business targeted for the period for each product or service, the competition and the number of calls made in the previous period. Add to this the calls planned in this period. As time progresses, indicate the number of calls made and leave space for comment on the net outcome. Figure 15 suggests an example of the form you might use.

This is mainly a personal tool for the sales team to help them construct their own forecasts, but you may also want to see copies at the end of each period to assess the effectiveness of the planning and the success rate.

Quotation record

For each sales territory, list every product across the top of the page and then note each prospect's name and the value quoted, month by month. Against each quote, a record of the outcome can then be made as time passes. This is an invaluable method not only for recording conversion rates, which can then be used for forecasting, but also for highlighting where follow-up calls are required. Clearly, computer analysis makes the task more easy than preparing such a record manually.

Market share trends/competitor vulnerability

Each month, every sales person is asked to complete a standard form listing all the customers won from and lost to each major competitor, to give a net balance of market-share movement. This information might come, in turn, from a more detailed sheet drawn up for each product, where each account is listed together with the reason for the movement, whether favourable

Figure 15: Prospect Planner

REGION:

REPRESENTATIVE:

PERIOD WEEK Nos

PROSPECT	ESTIMATED ANNUAL VALUE	PRODUCT/ SERVICE	COMPETITOR	NO. OF PREVIOUS CALLS	PLANNED CALLS	WEEK NUMBER													CALLS MADE	NO. OF UNPLANNED CALLS	COMMENTS
						1	2	3	4	5	6	7	8	9	10	11	12	13			
TOTALS																					

1 = INITIAL CALL   2 = RECALL   3 = SURVEY   4 = PENCIL QUOTE   5 = QUOTE FOLLOW-UP   6 = ORDER

Figure 16: Competitor Vulnerability

REGION: _____ REPRESENTATIVE: _____ XYZ Product _____ MONTH: _____

ACCOUNTS	ESTIMATED ANNUAL VALUE (£)	COMPETITOR	PRICE	DELIVERY	PRODUCT	SERVICE	SELLING	OTHERS
					REASON			
GAINED:								
TOTAL ACCOUNTS GAINED:								
LOST:								
TOTAL ACCOUNTS LOST:								

110

or otherwise. An example is given in Figure 16, labelled 'competitor vulnerability chart'.

The strategic and tactical benefits of doing this are obvious. Less apparent, such a chart also ensures that the reason for winning or losing any business is established by the sales force. For the system to work well, it then needs you as sales manager to ensure that the overall consolidated results are communicated back, and that your team knows you are doing something positive with the invaluable information obtained.

New business record

Unless you are very dominant in a mature market, you will expect your sales team to seek increased growth from winning new business. This requires special skills, which should not only be rewarded accordingly, but should also be monitored separately. Your computerised records might do this automatically for you, or you can use a form similar to Figure 17.

Competitor records

You should know as much about your competitors as you do your customers. In one place (preferably your office), you should record everything you can, including published financial results, product and price information, personnel, salaries paid, and your best view of each competitor's strengths and weaknesses. Against these you need to have a strategy which is fully communicated to your team.

Top 30 customers record

Keeping in mind the spirit of Pareto's Law, make a specific record of the largest customers in each region (say the top thirty). Plot sales progress meticulously against previous years; a simple example is provided in Figure 18 which you might expand by

Figure 17: New Business Record

REGION: _____ REPRESENTATIVE: _____ YEAR: _____

CUSTOMER	ESTIMATED ANNUAL VALUE	GAINED BY	YEAR-TO-DATE						CUMULATIVE SALES OF NEW BUSINESS						
			J	F	M	A	M	J	J	A	S	O	N	D

Figure 18: Top 30 Sales Comparisons – Summary

NO	CUSTOMER	YEAR-TO-DATE COMPARISON		COMMENTS
		19 – – – – LAST YEAR __ months	19 – – – – THIS YEAR __ months	
1				
2				
3				
4				
5				
6				
7				
8				
9				
10				
11				
12				
13				
14				
15				
16				
17				
18				
19				
20				
21				
22				
23				
24				
25				
26				
27				
28				
29				
30				

keeping a regular update of the number of sales and service visits made and competitor reaction. Bigger customers are always more difficult to replace, so guard this business jealously.

Other records

Other records which you will need to keep and monitor will include expenses (sales staff and other departmental costs), promotion activity and results, monthly reports, complaint records and credit given, free-of-charge samples and demonstration-equipment holdings, cost–price–profitability data, product sales trends, forward-order loads, credit limits and orders held pending payment, discount structures, agency commissions, bonus schemes, salary-progression records, job evaluations, and so on.

All record-keeping takes administrative time and records will proliferate if you let them. It is essential therefore to review these records regularly to ensure that the information they contain is both made available and used. Computers can help substantially – but make sure that the systems you have work well manually before automating them.

The more your systems are formalised, the easier your job becomes – and the easier it will be to hand over when you take your next well-earned promotion. And why should that be important? Because managers who make it hard for others to follow tend to make themselves indispensable; they are then rarely promoted because they are seen as being too difficult to replace.

11 Motivation and Reward

'The strength of a man's virtue should not be measured by his special exertions, but by his habitual acts.'

Blaise Pascal

What makes people want to work, apart from economic necessity? What makes them want to work harder? There are many theories about motivation at work and you will find study rewarding. Unfortunately, theory alone can at best only offer guidance to what is good practice, and at worst may confuse. People are of course all different, and what enthuses a young 'tiger' (or 'tigress') to go out and do the very best for you will almost certainly be different from that which will motivate someone much older; what works well in the USA may easily not work so well in the UK; what stimulates a single person to greater effort may be quite different for what applies to someone with family responsibilities, and so on.

Most people accept that money, on its own, can be a poor motivator for better work or greater effort. A boring job, bad management, disillusioned colleagues or lack of personal recognition may all dispirit the best-intentioned employee, however much you pay. Equally, you can find highly motivated, enthusiastic and loyal employees in companies which, frankly, pay very badly. Research indeed shows that most people rate a good salary some way behind security (which for many becomes increasingly important with age), job interest, challenge, appreciation and recognition.

Financial incentives

If you wish to motivate a team, the first step must still be to attend first to those aspects which might *demotivate*, called 'hygiene' or 'maintenance' factors by Fred Herzberg, who is worth reading on the subject. These factors, such as job status and conditions, responsibility and involvement, respect and recognition, are essential to the question of 'Why work here, rather than anywhere else?' As a manager you will need to attend to these hygiene factors by removing, wherever possible, those aspects which cause dissatisfaction.

The next step is to establish, once people *do* want to work 'here' rather than elsewhere, why they should wish or be prepared to work *harder*. You might expect that the answer is additional financial incentive, but it doesn't have to be. Promise of more responsibility and status, the challenge of meeting tough but achievable goals, or even the peer-group pressure that comes from team spirit, can all be powerful stimulants to greater effort.

However, money as a motivator clearly plays a major part for many people, as it is so directly instrumental in helping people to achieve personal goals of a material nature. Money also has the benefit of being unambiguously quantifiable by the recipient, and can therefore be used as a basis for comparison with others.

These are relevant thoughts in wrestling with the problem of how to reward a sales team and provide additional incentives. Some companies have done their own research to find out what works for their employees. You may well wish to do the same, noting the emphasis on what works for *your* team, rather than research on what other people might do.

There is a classic case study of a survey of dealers selling construction machinery and equipment in the USA. It was designed to establish the effectiveness of nine different reward schemes, ranging from salary only, to salary plus commission on either sales or gross profits, to salary plus some commission based on a quota and a bonus, to commission on total sales only. The results were most revealing, especially when the results of a recent survey by *Sales Direction Magazine* of actual practice in the UK are matched with the American research.

116

In the American study, the largest volumes were sold by those on **commission only,** but this scheme was the most expensive to operate. Note that such a scheme is often considered unreasonable in Europe because it guarantees no base income, although it certainly concentrates the mind. The UK survey showed that companies operating such a reward scheme suffer a very high staff turnover and, unlike the American survey, a relatively low sales revenue per sales person. It is not surprising therefore that the UK survey only found a mere 4 per cent of its sample companies to be using such a scheme.

At the other extreme, the American study found that payment by **salary alone** produced the lowest overall sales and, in this case, cost the most per unit of sale. In other words, no special financial motivation resulted in not very special results, as you might expect. Interestingly, the UK survey found that companies who used no commission scheme produced high sales revenues in the companies studied, particularly in the case of territorial sales teams (as opposed to key-account executives), and very low staff turnover. Such a pay scheme was shown to be particularly favoured by larger companies (over £100 million annual sales) and by 22 per cent of all companies surveyed. However, it is doubtful if such a reward scheme can, with its emphasis on stability and job security, realistically motivate sales teams to prospect for *new* business, especially in view of the greater sales skills and effort that new-business prospecting indubitably demands.

The American case study found that the best results in terms of the highest net profit produced for the dealers was a reward package based on **salary plus commission calculated on total sales.** It also produced the second highest sales volume. Further, the highest-paid sales representative in this instance, who was paid three times as much as the lowest-paid, sold five times as much. Interestingly, 51 per cent of the companies surveyed in the UK also use such a scheme. Sadly, the UK survey found little correlation between the details of any particular scheme and its success, as measured by sales revenue per sales person. The unhappy conclusion to be drawn is that often, however sophisticated the scheme – and many UK companies use a blend of commission schemes based on volume, margins, and other measures (such as working capital gauged by debtors and stock turnover) – the pay-back and effectiveness of financial incentives is badly managed.

Useful Exercise: Reward Survey

Establish what your competitors pay, in terms of salary, commisson and bonus, against what targets, and how often. Most managers are prepared to exchange such information in good faith but, if not, scan their recruitment advertisements and talk to recruitment agencies who operate in your field. Figure 19 gives an example of the data you might wish to record.

Now comes the difficult part: how do you relate the results to your company's culture? To do this successfully, you need an independent and unbiased view. It is important to know what your team feel about reward schemes, but it is most unlikely that you will get an objective view, from them alone, of what will produce the optimum results.

If you think the results of other companies which you survey are not likely to translate directly to your people, consider employing a professional to do this research for you.

Whatever reward scheme you choose, monitor the results carefully. Be prepared at regular intervals to review and amend the scheme in whatever way may be appropriate. Sophisticated bonus schemes are of little value if they do not produce the superior results you should rightly seek.

You need not be too concerned about the acceptance of periodic changes in the reward scheme by your team, *provided* that you tell them at the outset that the scheme is designed to pay superior sums for superior performance, and may therefore need to be changed in the light of changing circumstances. Note also that any scheme you adopt *must* be transparently fair, and meet the other criteria covered under *Commission and bonus*.

Salary

Salaries for sales staff can vary by at least a factor of ten, depending mainly of course upon the market and product, but also on success, age, location and experience. It is clearly important to establish the 'going rate' for your business sector and, with your other senior colleagues, decide on your company policy. Smaller

Figure 19: Competitors' Salaries

REGION: _____   COMPANY: _____   DATE: _____

OUR JOB TITLE	COMPETITOR EQUIVALENT	SALARY	PROFIT SHARE/ COMMISSION	CAR CHOICE AND PERIOD OF RENEWAL	LUNCH ALLOWANCE	OTHER BENEFITS
Service engineer						
Senior service engineer						
Sales engineer						
Senior sales engineer						
Section leaders/consultants						
Field sales manager						
Regional sales manager						
General sales manager						
UK sales manager						

119

companies may feel they do not need one: they will pay whatever it takes to recruit and retain the people they decide they want and can afford. Unfortunately, even for such companies, life rarely remains that simple. Before long, they will find that anomalies creep in. Someone will invariably be out of line with the others and soon the package which it was hoped would motivate the team will do the opposite.

Accordingly, it is good practice to set salary bands that reflect your policy, and which fairly reward superior performance and experience. There is no reason why everyone should be paid the same, but there should be good reasons – beyond mere chance – why people should be paid differently. If you operate a job-grading scheme, make sure that salaries between neighbouring grades overlap. Someone at a lower grade, performing well, might reasonably and rightfully expect to be paid more in some circumstances than a new entrant to a higher grade. In the longer term, as the new recruit begins to justify a higher grading, the balance will change, of course; but you need to be able to reward and retain good staff in all grades by such a mechanism.

The most frequent difficulty of a salary scheme occurs when you have to pay outside your agreed pay scale in order to attract the right calibre of applicants. It is rarely right to make special exceptions. If you have to amend your salary scales, you should seek to apply these new scales to your other employees as well, as soon as you can.

Commission and bonus

The choice between a variable commission rate and a fixed bonus payable once a pre-set target has been met, or even a combination of the two, should be made after a survey such as described in the useful exercise above. Your aim is to choose the most cost-effective result which meets your objectives. Once you have made your decision (and had it approved by your superior), there are some golden rules to apply:

- **Any scheme should be easy to understand and preferably easy to operate.** To work well, any scheme must allow for a regular feedback on performance. Your team needs to know exactly what they have to do at any given time to influence results so that they can realistically maximise their earnings. Consider converting annual targets, for example, into monthly objectives. Review performance regularly and be prepared to counsel new tactics when necessary.

- **The scheme must be fair and should not be heavily influenced by factors outside the control of the beneficiary.** For example, you need to agree who gets the recognition for an order which has been placed by a subsidiary in one area, but negotiated by someone else at the customer's parent company in a different region. Each member of the team must feel that their objectives are, as far as possible, really under their control.

- **Targets set should be achievable.** An unachievable goal will only demotivate, and of course devalue the whole scheme.

- **Set bonus or commission targets that truly reflect your company's objectives.** There is no point paying for extra sales that have unacceptably low margins, for example. If necessary, set different reward rates for different products. If a sales force has some influence on discount policy, consider deducting from the bonus or commission payable some or all of the margin given away this way.

- **Excellent results should be rewarded excellently.** If this means that someone exceeds all expectations and, under the rules of the scheme, ends up by being paid more than you, be pleased for both the individual concerned and the company. If you are unhappy with this, renegotiate your own bonus scheme!

- **Pay awards promptly.** The incentive soon diminishes in its effect if the reward arrives long after the event. Consider making part of the scheme payable monthly, if you can administrate this effectively.

121

- **Make sure that the reward is large enough to be a genuine incentive but not so large that, if the target is not met, personal bankruptcy or mortgage foreclosure looms.** Many companies feel that somewhere around 20–30 per cent of base salary is a good on-target compromise. Less, and it may not stimulate. More, and it may warp commercial judgement as to what is sensible, especially if failure to achieve targets might then cause financial hardship.

In the short term, maladministration of salaries and reward schemes can be the biggest single source of dissatisfaction for a sales team, after the company car policy. In the longer term, it can be *the* largest source, so tread with care.

Apart from satisfying your team's needs, there is an equally important consideration: make sure that the financial rewards made this way also benefit your company's performance. If you cannot produce an effective scheme, you may just do better by not having one at all. In the survey already reported by Industrial Market Research Ltd, *How British Industry Sells*, 50 per cent of companies surveyed had no bonus or commission scheme for their sales people.

Other incentives

Cash need not be the only reward mechanism at your disposal. We have already noted that public recognition of an excellent performance is an important factor in motivating people, and this is especially so for many sales teams. Methods of recognising outstanding results can range from a simple PR exercise, where successful colleagues are rewarded by the recognition and acclaim of internal publicity (such as notice-boards and news-sheets), to competitions and league tables where the reward may be more tangible, such as an exotic holiday in the Bahamas, for example. A study by *Sales Direction Magazine* showed that in the UK as many as one company in five uses competitions. Note, however, that these should be truly cost-effective incentives and not just a jamboree for the boss's blue-eyed boys (or girls). Competitions need very careful planning and research, and transparent fairness, to succeed.

A traditional incentive used in the past has been the 'chairman's bottle', often awarded discreetly just before Christmas at the whim of senior management. As an incentive, it may work well initially, but it can have dangerous repercussions. Come the next year, last year's lucky recipients will begin to expect a gift as of right, and it will then no longer be an incentive. Worse, they may be passed over next year, when they will wonder what they did wrong. It can then become a decided disincentive. Altogether, such initiatives may be born out of good intentions, but will usually end in metaphorical tears. An indiscriminate box of chocolates or turkey presented at Christmas-time to every representative's partner, with expressions of thanks for their support and contribution over the year, may be much more appropriate. Even then, you need to be careful about the bachelors and spinsters in your team, not to mention any who may have suffered divorce or bereavement.

Short and specific competitions from time to time, designed to focus on a particular short-term goal, can be much more effective in terms of promoting special effort. The aim could be to win the most new accounts, to sell the most units of a specific product or service, or to move slow-moving stock. Make the goals fair and publish interim results regularly and publicly. If it is done well, the sense of rivalry can be most stimulating. Involve *all* those involved, including sales-office and support staff. This can be an excellent way to build team spirit in the long term, and achieve some immediate objectives in the shorter term.

Commitment

Another aspect of motivation should also be considered, relating back to leadership. Successful sales people are often self-driven, independent and necessarily resilient. It is accordingly easy to forget that even the best sales teams need to be forged into a *team*, and that their motivational needs must be attended to. Setting clear and consistent objectives, providing regular feedback of the results, together with praise and applause when it is due, certainly helps. But there is more to motivation than that.

It is also important to develop a spirit of commitment to the company, which must come from the top, and a positive attitude that only the best will do and all things are possible.

In addition to this, people in your team must feel that their views and comments are listened to, carefully, and acted upon when appropriate. When objectives are set, the team must feel some sense of personal ownership of these objectives, which can only be acquired if the whole team has played a part in the decision-making. We look at this in the next section.

12 Forecasting and Budgets

'The best qualification of a prophet is to have a good memory.'

Lord Halifax – before computers

If it is true that a successful company thrives on making carefully thought-out plans and executing them, then it follows that the ability to quantify the likely results of these plans must play an essential part in this success. There is an established management attitude here which is to be applauded:

- If something adverse is going to happen in the market-place (such as a decline in demand or the closure of a major customer), a manager cannot be criticised if the event was forecast, or at least prepared for as a contingency.

- It is a failure, however, *not* to forecast a significant event if it could have been foreseen, or at least prepared for.

A requirement of most business leaders – and of the Stock Exchange and other investors – is 'Give us no surprises'. The problem is that quite sophisticated forecasts, based on a full array of statistical techniques, can often go wrong. While this is especially so in complex macroeconomic models, such as those used to predict demand for electricity, for example, or road usage, false pictures can also be produced just as readily on a much smaller scale. This last is especially true of smaller companies who try to use statistical techniques on inadequate data.

This is not to say that mathematical treatment of as much relevant data as can be found (including the monitoring of trends

'A manager cannot be criticised if the event was forecast, or at least prepared for.'

by moving averages (see Figure 3), regression analysis, etc.) should be discouraged. Rather, subjective evaluation of the predictions should also be included, applying as much common sense as you can muster. Some companies go in for statistical analysis which is far too complex and can grossly outweigh its usefulness.

The foundation of a successful sales forecast must be a data base of past order patterns and present enquiry levels. Only by knowing how your sales team have performed in today's market can you realistically forecast how they will perform in tomorrow's. This is where your base data on all the key management ratios, discussed in the last section under *Key ratios* and *Reporting systems*, become so valuable, including your sales performance record, the prospect planner, the prospect bank, quotation records and so on. They are designed to help forecasting and are an essential aid.

Only after examining and understanding *current* activities is it then realistic to look at economic and other 'external' trends, together with specific sales and marketing intiatives that you are planning ahead, in order to forecast *future* sales.

Business planning

Forecasting needs to offer more than a glimpse into the shorter-term future. It should also provide the basis for your company's longer-term business planning. There appears to be a wide variety of methods in use, and you need to be aware of them.

A recent and most instructive survey of 570 companies in the UK, Canada and West Germany, by the Department of Marketing at the University of Manitoba, revealed as many as nine different methods in popular use. Section 'e' of Figure 20 summarises this. (Don't worry now about some of the 'marketing components' listed in section 'h'. They are explained in the next section, 'Marketing', and form an invaluable check-list for your own planning activities.)

One of the methods that appears to produce the best results, although not as frequently used as one might expect, is described as being **Top down – bottom up**. This means that a sense of

127

Figure 20: How Businesses Plan

What percentage of companies:	UK	CANADA	W. GERMANY
a) Have informal planning procedures.	25	21	27
b) Use a formal planning routine.	52	57	56
c) Take 6–12 weeks to plan.	65	43	51
d) Have plans for more than one year.	72	66	64
e) Use the following methods:			
1) Marketing dept led.	25	31	14
2) Product manager led.	11	10	6
3) Top down.	12	1	4
4) Bottom up.	6	7	6
5) Top down–Bottom up.	6	1	9
6) Informal. React as necessary.	8	5	3
7) Delegate to individuals.	4	7	0
8) Top states strategy, plan is developed lower down.	3	7	9
9) Top sets performance goals, tactics developed lower down.	2	4	5
f) Have marketing plan only.	28	27	14
g) Have marketing and corporate plan,	61	62	63
– and marketing plan comes first,	10	18	28
– or corporate plan comes first,	30	28	15
– or both are done together.	52	40	46
h) Use the following 'components' in their marketing plans:			
Forecast market demand	70	67	66
Current market share	64	59	57
Share of competition	52	45	60
Competitive strengths/weakness	64	61	72
Consider market segmentation	54	46	60
Changing needs of customer	66	52	57
Technological trends	20	26	43
Appraise risk factors	38	25	38
Environmental issues	13	13	24
Government regulatory issues	20	22	21
Consider alternative strategies	23	26	32
Use portfolio management	25	22	33
Use product life-cycle analysis	26	15	18
Post-mortem past plans	21	24	31
State objectives	82	78	85
Set action plans	73	77	84
Develop contingency plans	20	16	18

(Study by M. D. Beckman and P. McDonald, University of Manitoba) strategic direction in line with overall business objectives must first be set by the senior management (i.e. 'Top down'). This provides the strategic direction for the next stage. Detailed sales forecasts can then be prepared from the grass roots of the sales team upwards (i.e. 'Bottom up'), in line with these objectives.

This needs to be an iterative process, because the implications of the first 'Bottom up' forecast may well be at variance with your production resources, financial goals, or other objectives. Equally, a market sector may exhibit longer-term trends which your sales team may well not be aware of, but you should be. These market trends also need to be applied, if only to give a weighting to the overall credibility of the plan you construct. For example, if your sales team forecasts a cumulative 15 per cent rise in volume and yet all the economic indicators point to an imminent recession, you will probably want to go back and re-evaluate your forecast.

One of the principal benefits of such a planning routine is that all levels of management are involved. This not only means that all issues can be considered, but it also allows for a healthy degree of commitment through participation. No one can complain that they were not consulted. Such a method also ensures that all elements of the plan are mutually compatible, while still allowing senior management the possibility of exercising a veto if necessary.

The overall business planning cycle might therefore look something like Figure 21, top down and bottom up. The full cycle will also integrate the promotion and advertising activities, and of course a review of the personnel demands, purchasing plans, technical development activities, plus a full expense budget.

The planning period may cover just one year, but it is usually wiser to plan for one year in detail and perhaps the next two years in more general terms. That way, longer-term objectives and trends can be taken care of. At the end of each year, performance against last year's detailed plan should be reviewed before preparing the next year's plan. One year further ahead should then be added to the overall long-term projection. Some companies prefer to take an even longer view, of say five years, but experience shows

129

Figure 21: Typical Business Planning Cycle

Phase 1	**CORPORATE OBJECTIVES:**
	Return on capital employed target
	Return on sales target
	Cash generation and investment

Phase 2	**MARKETING OBJECTIVES:**
	Growth targets
	Market-share objectives
	Market-segment targets
	New-product development

Phase 3	**THE SALES PLAN:**
	Detailed sales forecast by
	customer and product, showing
	movement in both volume and sales
	price, phased for each month

Phase 4	**PRODUCTION PLAN:**
	Detailed review of
	production/service resources
	required to meet the sales plan

Phase 5	**FINANCIAL BUDGET:**
	The company's financial operating
	statement based on all of the above,
	phased by reporting period (e.g. week,
	month or quarter), presented as a
	target set of accounts for the budget
	period, by which to monitor actual
	performance

130

that any predictions over such an extended period of time rarely justify the extra work entailed, because of the scale of uncertainty involved at the operating level.

Once a detailed annual budget has been set, it is of course important to keep the actual performance under review. If there are any major changes to the assumptions made, revised forecasts may be necessary. Note however that it is usually good practice still to monitor performance against the original rather than the revised budget, if only to highlight the importance of accurate budgeting and forecasting in the first instance.

(Note the accent on **financial goals,** which drive corporate objectives in the business-planning procedure described above. This is a clear demonstration of the powerful influence that investors often exert on strategic planning in the West, with the prime goal being steady profit growth and return on capital. So how do companies budget in Japan? Judging from the present-ation of their annual reports, their planning process starts with, and focuses on, the *market-place* (i.e. customer needs, service and market share, new products and markets). Only *after* the market objectives are set is the necessary financial support determined. You may well feel that *this* is true market orientation!)

The sales manager's role in the budget process is clear. One of his most important tasks is to apply a filter to what each member of the sales team has committed him or herself to, in building up the overall target. Contrary to expectation perhaps, given that sales bonuses will usually be measured against these sales predictions, experience shows that the inclination of most sales teams is to forecast *more* ambitiously than is realistic, rather than less. It is here that your judgement and panoramic over-view should come into play, taking into account all the general economic indicators that are available to you. If you do revise a particular sales target, however, you should only do so after full discussion with the individual concerned. Equally, bonuses should only apply to the final targets set; not those initially proposed by the sales team.

Apart from taking a hard look at what each member of the team is proposing to forecast, by customer and product, it is also an important duty of the sales manager to be closely aware of what

'The inclination of most teams is to forecast more ambitiously than is realistic.'

board-level expectations are. The last thing you want is to find yourself having to resist pressures from above, to forecast better sales than you think are realistic, for example. Resist these pressures you must, but it is much better to influence your superiors' expectations *ahead* of a formal presentation of your predictions, rather than afterwards.

Strategic considerations

You will readily appreciate from all that has gone before that excelling as a sales manager requires much more than basic tactical sales skills. For example, this book has repeatedly shown how important strategic planning skills separate the adequate manager from the excellent one.

The dividing line between sales and marketing has always been subject to dispute. Once, the sales manager was master and the marketing team either non-existent, or a humble servant. Then the better marketing teams demonstrated the power of their longer-range strategic skills and in some business sectors the sales team became the lackeys of the marketing generals. Unfortunately, some marketing strategists lost sight of the day-to-day war raging in the market-place. They became closeted in an ivory tower of generalities and theory, so that some sales teams found themselves with the powerful argument that if the company did not look after today's sales needs, there would be no tomorrow for the marketers to worry about.

So the balance between the functions has oscillated. In hard times, the marketing team has been the easiest overhead to cut. In other periods of company stagnation, it has needed a radical change of market emphasis – led by a visionary marketing team – to produce a vital change of direction and business rejuvenation, which has then restored the power of marketing in the land.

Independently of economic swings, personalities and internal politics, however, it has always been clear to the more successful companies – and reinforced by all the published research – that the ideal balance should be an intimate blend of both sales and marketing skills. A successful company needs both, and the teams that work well together generally produce the best results.

Accordingly, a successful sales manager needs to be as aware of marketing disciplines as a marketing team needs to be sensitive to the skills which a professional sales team can bring to bear. It is with no apologies therefore that your attention is addressed to the next section on marketing.

III

MARKETING

'Good Marketing is a function of good customers.'
'Marketing capabilities are more important than good products.'

P. Spillard

13   What is Marketing?

Marketing may be a discipline to be learned, but it is also an attitude of mind to be absorbed. To acquire a true marketing orientation, it is of course important to learn the tools of the trade, but there is also the important matter of 'feel'. Marketing is not just a mechanical instrument, to be used when required. It should also be a spirit which permeates *all* of your commercial thinking and strategic direction.

Marketing has been described as 'customer creation' and 'what makes selling possible'. Both statements are true, yet miss the central truth. Marketing is about understanding. For example: what are the dynamics of your market-place, your customers and your competitors? Which markets do you want to serve and what are their features? How big are they, what share do you have and how much *could* you have? How price/quality/delivery-sensitive is each market? What do your prospective customers need, and what is it worth to them to get it? How well do your products and services meet these needs, and how do you want to be positioned in the market-place relative to the competition? How are you to promote your company and its products to customers and prospects most cost-effectively? How is all this to be translated into long-term profit growth? These are the challenges of marketing.

Marketing versus selling

Sadly, selling as an occupation has historically been held in low esteem. Let us hope that greater professionalism is changing this view. Nevertheless, in order to avoid describing people as 'salesmen', there is a tendency to use misleading terms such as 'marketing executives' – which is admittedly better than the old-fashioned term, no longer heard, of 'commercial traveller'. This bowdlerising of job titles completely obscures the fundamental differences between selling and marketing, even if there is no reason why sales people should not recognise they are part of a marketing team, and vice versa.

The major differences between marketing and selling can be described as follows:

- If selling is the *tactical* expression of a commercial enterprise, then marketing provides the *strategy* that underlies it.

- Selling may in essence be devoted to ensuring that customers buy what a company offers. Marketing ensures that companies offer what customers want.

The Seven Ps of marketing

It is helpful to keep in mind the complete package of the basic elements of marketing as a useful check-list, the so-called 'Seven Ps'. We shall look at each of these elements of marketing in more detail later, but in summary they are:

1) **Planning.** This covers basic market research through to forecasting, trend analysis and monitoring, all as a foundation stone to establishing business strategy and sales goals.

2) **Promotion.** Often, marketing is confused with advertising, which is only one form of promoting products and services in the market-place. The general public may be more aware of advertising as a promotional tool, but there are many other methods of promoting a product, service or company, which may often be more cost-effective. In turn, promotion is only part of marketing.

3) **Product (including Services).** What is on offer, and how well does it meet customers' needs? This section includes the management of a product portfolio, new-product development, design, quality and performance, as well as the study of life-cycles and how to manipulate them.

4) **Position.** What is the market's perception of your company and its products, and how does this compare with your own view? The position a product holds in a market-place can be altered, but first it is necessary to understand what that position is. One method is to split the market into unique categories, a powerful technique known as market segmentation.

5) **Pricing.** Your pricing strategy will depend on many factors, including your broad strategic objectives and the product's perceived value in your chosen markets. Pricing tends to be a much more sophisticated issue than many sales managers would allow.

6) **Placement.** This is about the road to market: i.e. distribution. It covers the role of agents, wholesalers and retailers, as well as more mundane but equally important considerations such as transport and shipping.

7) **Packaging.** In some markets, packaging can be an integral part of the product offering, in others a forgotten necessity. It not only covers product protection and covering, and even mandatory labelling when relevant, but also the visual appeal of what is inside. Packaging can also refer to the collection of features that you assemble, related to your product or service, which distinguishes your place in the market relative to others.

14 Planning

'Time spent in good reconnaissance is never wasted.'
Military maxim, forgotten by General Custer and the 7th Cavalry

We have already covered much ground on the subject of planning in earlier chapters, particularly in the contexts of trend analysis, forecasting and monitoring of results, as well as of matching resources to objectives. Planning should be meat and drink to both a sales and a marketing function.

Market research

Market research, being part of the planning effort, is a formal name for what many of your sales people will be doing as one of their routine tasks anyway – or at least should be. However, market research is more than simple intelligence-gathering. What makes it so valuable is not the knowledge itself, but of course what you do with the information when you have gathered it.

You might be surprised at how much valuable information will be available from your own customer records. For example, quite sophisticated marketing plans can be built up from the skilled analysis of just your customers' post codes. With this basic information alone, and probably the help of some computer analysis, much important information can be produced on your customers' geographic distribution. Match this to your call plans and you have a very powerful tool for optimising journey-planning. If you sell to the public, post codes can also give

140

invaluable guidance on buying habits, socio-economic class, 'life-styles' and so on.

To obtain the fullest benefits of market research, and its broader cousin marketing research, very specific but trainable skills are required. If your team does not possess these skills, have no compunction about hiring them from outside as and when you need them.

The most frequent use of market research is probably the quantification of market size, market share and future trends for existing activities. However, market research should also be an essential part – at the earliest possible moment – of any new-product development or acquisition study. Many companies forget or forgo this essential stage of any *new* market activity: it is then not surprising that many new ventures subsequently fail. Expert advice and research in the planning stages of any new venture can be worth their weight in gold in terms of anguish saved later on.

Market research can also offer other benefits, such as reflecting the image of a company in the market-place, estimating the effectiveness of promotional activities (it can provide vital pre-emptive advice in this area), and gauging the market position of the competition or the likely effects of new legislation or tech-nology. Many of these issues can most usefully be summarised in a SWOT analysis – a valuable way to commence any strategic planning initiative.

SWOT

This stands for Strengths, Weaknesses, Opportunities and Threats, and is an analysis that should be done not just for your own company, but for all your principal competitors. A study of your **strengths** should lead to the identification of a number of **opportunities,** which your business plan should in turn highlight, indicating how they will be capitalised upon. Equally, an analysis of your company **weaknesses** and the **threats** to which it is exposed will also be needed. Many of the threats you are exposed to will be potential opportunities, and the intention of such a planning exercise must be to ensure that these opportunities are realised too.

Useful Exercise: SWOT analysis

If you haven't already done so, gather a few senior colleagues together and do your own SWOT analysis. If you need help in doing this, consider recruiting outside professional advice.

When you have listed all the strengths and weaknesses of your company and its products, together with the opportunities and threats in the market-place, decide what you now need to do. In constructing the necessary action list that should then follow, allocate the responsibility for each action to a named individual, specify the time-scale for review that has been agreed, and draw up any expenditure budget that may be required.

The action list should be reviewed regularly. The worst fate of any such planning exercise is for the report to lie in the bottom of someone's drawer, which sadly happens all too often.

---

15 Promotion

'Perception is reality.'

Advertising aphorism

Many companies advertise, issue glossy corporate brochures, take part in exhibitions, give away trade gifts and so on, for no better reason than because their competitors do. This may provide a rich living for the promotions industry, but such an attitude is a waste of hard-earned profit by those who spend in such an ill-disciplined and unplanned manner.

Promotion can be **internal,** to inform and possibly encourage your own colleagues; **local,** to demonstrate what a responsible and exciting employer your company is to work for; or, most commonly, **external,** with the aim of giving customers and prospects 'favourable product awareness'. In this last context, one of the most important roles of promotion is to warm up your prospective market *before* the sales team make direct contact. There is nothing worse than for a sales person to be greeted by 'I do not know you, I do not know your company, nor do I know your products. Now, *what* was it you wanted to sell to me?' As the old marketing saw has it, 'Never sell to strangers'!

Promotion can cover leaflets, data sheets and catalogues; seminars and exhibitions; press releases, editorial coverage and direct mail; advertising and trade gifts; sponsorship and even charitable donations. Behind all this effort, which can be very costly and time-consuming, there needs to be a strategy.

One of the best ways to use these promotional tools is in the context of that elderly but still highly serviceable mnemonic, 'AIDA'. As you will surely know, this stands for:

Attention–Interest–Desire–Action,

and describes the route any sales person will want to take to win the order. Until the prospect's *attention* has been engaged, selling cannot start. However, to proceed further, there must be good reason for the prospect to find some *interest* in the proposition or the attention gained will soon be lost. However, every sales person knows that interest is not enough to win the sale. The prospect must need (or '*desire*') ownership of the product or service in question, and yours in particular. Thereafter, for the sale to be concluded, the deal must be closed. In other words, the prospect needs to take *action*, and place an order.

Given that these steps are traditional routes a company needs to follow to make a sale, the problem for many companies is that they expect their sales team to cover all of these steps on their own. This is a huge waste of money and time. It is this waste that a good promotional activity should be designed to save, particularly at the beginning.

A much more cost-effective route to gaining attention could be, rather than to send your expensive sales team on costly prospecting trips, to promote your product and company by advertising, well-constructed mail shots and so on. In some cases, these initiatives might work the complete sales cycle for you without a single sales call. For more complex propositions, however, there will be detailed questions to answer; this is where exhibitions, good literature and technical data sheets can come into play in order to generate interest, and even desire. Only then might it be appropriate to employ your crack sales team, to close the deal either by direct customer visits or possibly by seminars and road-shows. A conceptual diagram showing this relationship between promotional activity and making the sale is shown in Figure 22.

Promotions expertise is a big and skilled field, but there are one or two comments worth highlighting here for all sales managers.

Advertising

Many an advertising agency will tell you that advertising can often be likened to wetting one's pants. If you will excuse the crudity of

Figure 22: The Relationship Between Promotion and Sales

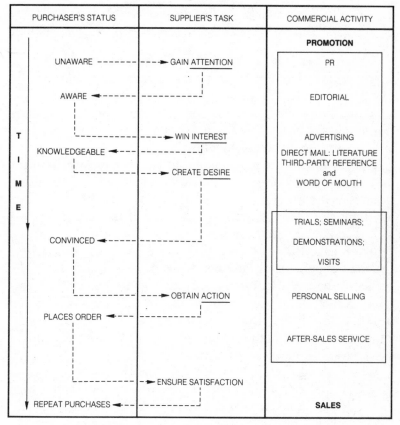

the analogy, they will tell you that initially it may make you feel warm and comfortable. But it won't take long before you will wish you hadn't; meanwhile, nobody else will know what you have done.

The rule should be that you should only advertise when you are totally clear what the message is, who the target is, and what outcome you can expect. Even then, the outcome you expect should be valued against the cost. Avoid rigorously any plea to advertise because your competitors do, or because you chairman thinks some publicity would be 'a good thing', unless you also are convinced that the exercise is worth while. If the exercise doesn't make money for your company somewhere along the line, don't do it (at least, that way) again. And always monitor the results.

What makes for a successful advertisement? Position is nearly always more important than size of spread or multiplicity of colour. People will always look at a picture before reading a headline, but while a headline does not need a picture, an illustration always needs a headline. If you use both, the headline and picture should complement each other.

The headline is the most important part of any advertisement and therefore requires the greatest thought. Consider using phrases that start Why . . . ? or How . . . ? or Who . . . ?, or anything else that will grab the attention of the reader, as long as it is legal and decent, honest and true. Text should be short, pithy and factual, with plenty of white space. A good advertisement should nearly always demand some action from the reader at the end. Because most readers go to the bottom right-hand corner of a page after taking in any picture and the headline, that is the place for your company or product's name. Finally, review whether your ad has achieved your initial objectives. If it hasn't, start again!

Where should one advertise? Ask for the latest readership data from the journal in question, or look at a publication such as the *British Rate and Data* (*BRAD*) which will tell you, and calculate how much it costs to reach the audience of interest to you. Ask your sales force what their customers read, and what enjoys their respect. As always, monitor the results!

Exhibitions

Overseas, much business is traditionally conducted at trade fairs and exhibitions, but in the UK this is less so. The best reason for exhibiting in the UK is when you have something new to offer. Otherwise, think again.

You don't have to attend the very large, prestigious and expensive shows to win your much-sought-after leads. Some of the most cost-effective exhibitions are table-top stands in hotels, where a small number of other companies can exhibit with parallel but non-competing products to a selected audience.

Whatever the size of the show, be sure to present your exhibits and the company in the best possible light. Many companies find that exhibition space often costs more than they would like, and accordingly try and save on stand design. This is usually a mistake; aisle frontage is important and a bad position can be disadvantageous, but a poor overall presentation is just crazy. If you cannot present a favourable image, it is better to present none at all. With this in mind, try to have a part of the stand covered from view, so that briefcases and clutter can be kept out of sight. Appoint a stand manager, and make it a requirement that all dirty coffee-cups, glasses or plastic beakers are removed as soon as they are finished with.

Having decided to attend an exhibition, you will obviously want as many interested visitors as possible. Rather than wait for them to turn up, tell them in advance that you will be exhibiting. Nearer the time, send them entry tickets, travel instructions and so on. Meanwhile, make sure that you have organised a rota for stand duties and ensure that every member of the team has been properly trained. Not only should this mean knowing the detail of all the products on show and what literature you will have available to support them, it also means knowing how to approach a prospect. ('Are you interested in seeing the most reliable widget in the world, sir?' has to be better than the weak 'May I help you?', which all too often invites the answer 'No!')

Finally, ensure that *no one* visits your stand without note being taken of the visitor's name and job title, company name and address, and the nature of their interest. Then, having ensured that all enquiries can be properly logged, make sure that action is taken to follow up these hard-won enquiries, quickly and professionally. If you do all these things well, you will be a company in a thousand. Most don't!

147

Product literature

Catalogues tend to grow like weeds, unplanned and unloved. Yours should be precious flowers, well tended and much sought after.

Any range of catalogues should look as though they came from the same organisation. It is never too late to decide on a house style, but once you have, keep to it religiously for as long as it works for you. Whatever the item you choose to promote, establish at the beginning what the task of this particular piece of literature should be, and then keep this in the forefront of your mind. Good promotional literature should produce an end result – preferably enquiries and orders. If what you plan doesn't expressly ask the reader to take some action at the end, then reconsider its value.

The most frequent mistake people make in designing literature is that they think their prospects will read every word. You should be so lucky! Have as little text as you can possibly get away with, make key points boldly and succinctly, and use as many pictures, diagrams and 'white spaces' as you can.

Useful Exercise: Literature review

Collect a copy of every single piece of your company's literature that goes to customers. While you are at it, include letterheads, labels, invoices and quotation forms. Do they have a uniform style and presentation? What is each item's objective, and is it met? If you are not happy, do NOT attack the problem piecemeal. Get your senior colleagues to agree that your company has a problem and consider asking for some expert advice to upgrade your image. Unless you are very short of cash, do not attempt to address the problem yourself. Everyone likes an enthusiastic amateur, but people prefer to buy from enthusiastic professionals.

Press relations

Smaller companies often think of PR work as being applicable only to their larger brethren. This is not the case. Many editors are indeed submerged by puffy, poorly presented hand-outs, but they are always short of good, factual stories that inform in an interesting way. As most editorial coverage is free, it is surprising that more companies do not make better use of it.

The secret is partly in the story, partly in the presentation.

It should go without saying (but it doesn't) that your story *must* be of interest to the readership of the magazine, journal or newspaper. Preferably, it should also be newsworthy. Items for consideration should not only include new products, major new orders or new appointments, but perhaps also interesting visitors to your company, novel applications for your products, difficult problems solved and so on. 'Little and often' is usually preferable to an occasional and long-winded story. Few editors have the space.

If you look for interesting product or company news, you will be pleasantly surprised at how many items you will find. The skill is then to drip-feed these stories to the editors of those publications which your prospects will read. If you are not sure what these publications are, ask your sales force to find out.

The rules for presenting a good story are simple. Make sure that you have a clear beginning, a middle and an end. Give the story a strong but simple headline and finish by saying where the story has come from and who can provide additional information. On the basis that a picture tells a thousand words, always endeavour to include a professionally taken (i.e. focused!) black and white photograph, which must *always* carry your company name and a short caption (or the story headline) on the back. If at all possible, get the shot to include some human interest; a good application photograph is invariably better than a studio product-shot.

Having sent off your story, monitor the take-up by each magazine or journal (a press-cuttings agency can help you do this) and measure the response from each one. Don't forget to let your sales force know what stories you have released, and who has carried them in their pages, and plan carefully how you will reply to the interest aroused in your market-place. If you are disappointed in the take-up of a story, don't be bashful in contacting some of the editors you have mailed and ask for their advice. The better you can get to know the editors of the journals which are important to you, the more likely they will be to take and publish further stories from you.

Trade directories

It is a lucky sales manager who will not be pestered regularly with requests to take ever bigger and bolder displays in yet more trade directories. Some of these directories may well have their role to play for your company, but many will probably not. Decide on your policy, construct a budget and keep to it. Then monitor the results and prune ruthlessly next year.

In particular, be very wary of some overseas directories which send pseudo-invoices for orders that have never in fact been placed: insist that no invoices are paid by your company without you or a senior colleague approving them. Also, do not be fooled by other knavish tricks which will include 'We send out a copy to every embassy/library/Joe Soap' (will this really be of benefit to you, and who is running your marketing effort anyway?); 'We are about to go to print and have a last-minute cancellation. Your competitor XYZ has taken some space, by the way' (oh yes? If you are really tempted, check it out carefully, but do not allow yourself to be rushed); and 'Take just x more entries and we can give you a y per cent discount' – as with all the other approaches, you are being asked to spend more money than you planned. Consider the proposition, of course, but once you have laid your plans for the year, keep to them – or find a bottomless purse.

Gifts and calendars

Once, it was traditional to give lavish gifts, at Christmas-time in particular. Many a sales force would have their sales managers believe that it is still true; but it isn't. Small gifts may have a place in your promotional strategy, but contemplate first whether the overall spend that you plan could be directed elsewhere more

'Once, it was traditional to give lavish gifts, at Christmas-time in particular.'

efficiently. If small trade gifts, diaries and calendars are part of your promotional mix, make sure that they are of good quality and that they will carry your name *in the working environment* for the whole of next year. If not, desist.

By the way, on the subject of 'girlie' calendars: if in doubt, say 'No', unless your market totally and unambiguously demands them, and you can provide them without giving the appearance of running a brothel (unless, of course, you do . . .). And 'gifts' that verge on corruption? – see under *Bribery* later on!

Direct mail

With the increasing availability of computerisation, sophisticated data-base management and desk-top publishing, the use of mail shots to promote your company and its wares becomes increasingly attractive as a cost-effective promotional tool. If you need help, there are many outside sources of assistance, not the least of which are the postal services.

In using direct mail, be sure to guard against contributing to the increasing amount of badly researched, poorly targeted 'junk mail' which is in danger of devaluing this powerful aid. Decide what your goals are, screen your mailing list very carefully, and then be sure to plan the *whole* campaign, not forgetting that you need to plan the follow-up to your endeavours, as well as the mail shot itself.

16 Product

'There is nothing easier than selling to the public – nor more difficult than satisfying them.'

I. Adams

For 'product', read also 'service' and anything else a customer might buy from you. Now consider this.

Your livelihood, and that of all your colleagues, is dependent upon having products that your identified customers want to buy, not what your company wants to offer. This means paying attention to good design, performance, quality, delivery and price. While it is everyone's responsibility to get all these aspects right, the best people to judge the success or otherwise of your product are those who have the closest contact with the market. Second only to your customers, this means you and your sales team. If you do not feel that your product meets market requirements, you have a duty to say so. Forget the sensitivities of your production or technical colleagues. If you do not speak out, you are guilty of condoning a company myth that could eventually close you down. If the Emperor has no clothes on, you must say so.

New-product development

New ventures are bound to have some risk attached, but no new development at all can mean stagnation and eventual death. To reduce the risks, first spend as much time and money as you can on researching what the market needs. If this sounds obvious, consider what most people do. They regularly spend their money on developing a 'better' product without considering whether the market will actually want it – or pay for it. Researching the market means more than establishing current and future needs. It also means estimating likely benefits, price sensitivity, frequency of demand and overall market worth. Don't forget the competition, either. What are they up to, and how are they likely to react?

The next point to keep in mind about developing new products is that of timescale. For whatever reason, it always takes longer to develop a marketable product than is ever envisaged at the outset. As a consequence, the next most important stage (after market research) is also regularly short-changed: field testing.

New products are fragile things: get them not quite right to start with and you may never have another chance. Unfortunately, new-product development often incurs so much cost (and emotion) that there is every pressure to launch before the product is fully tested. Set this pressure against many development teams' inherent commitment to producing a 'perfect product' – so perfect it never sees the light of day – and you can see that there has to be a fine balance of commercial judgement on when to launch. But if in doubt, launch a little late rather than too early.

Finally, when you do launch, milk the opportunity for all it is worth, with pride and pizzazz. Build up a launch dossier for your sales team, to cover the product details, its features and benefits, the target market, pricing strategy, anticipated competition and delivery details. Spend time training and encouraging your sales team, because not even the best products 'sell themselves', as you surely know. Use every promotional tool available to you in advance to warm up the market, and then make sure that the product is available in adequate volume. There is nothing more frustrating to a team than to have a brand-new baby, and to have to ask people to wait to see it.

Two other points about new products. First, recognise that if the new product displaces an old one, you will need to run down your stocks of the old product first before you launch the new one, or they will hang around for ever. Secondly, don't forget that a new product is an excellent means of boosting the sales of your traditional lines as well.

Product life-cycle

Once any product has been around for some while, you will need to attend to its life-cycle. This will classically consist of an introductory phase, a period of consistent growth during market development, followed by market saturation and sales stagnation, and eventual decay (see Figure 23). Some products last as little as a few months, others for decades, but these do not have to be immutable facts of life.

Figure 23: The Product Life-Cycle – and How to Extend It

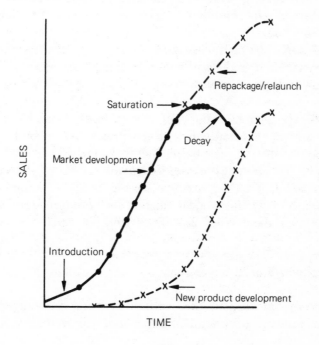

A life-cycle can be extended by having a newer product to launch as the market reaches saturation, or even by further modification or repackaging of the old product, so as to give it a new lease of life. The latter can be the cheaper way, and can extend a product's sales life-time for many years.

Useful Exercise: Product life-cycles

Do you know where your own products stand in their life-cycle? Plot each product's historical sales against time to find out. If there are any nearing maturity, you need to act quickly. Talk to your colleagues and see what you can do by way of repackaging the old product and developing new ones.

Product withdrawal

Eventually, even the best-loved products must be withdrawn one day, as sales decline. Leaving a market requires as careful attention as entering one.

It is amazing how many customers, who once appeared so reluctant to buy your fading product, blench at the thought that you might now withdraw it. If this is indeed your plan, attend to these sensitivities early on or else you will leave some very disgruntled customers. One way is to take them into your confidence as early as possible. If you cannot convert a customer to your new product, then you have no option but to use the price button and make the old one ever more expensive. In fact, some companies claim that their best products are those which customers refused to see die, in spite of huge price increases. It makes one wonder whether such products were priced too cheaply in their earlier days. They probably were!

Product portfolio management

Larger companies in particular, with extensive product ranges, will need to be aware of the relative strengths of their product range so that management and sales resources can be properly allocated. There is no point in retaining weak products if they take management effort away from the more attractive ones.

The strength of a product can be measured a number of ways. A classic approach developed by the Boston Consulting Group is to position products on a matrix grid, for example plotting market growth against relative market share as in Figure 24. A product with market share in a growing market is clearly a **star**, to be cherished and nurtured. A product that enjoys a high market

Figure 24: Product Portfolio Management

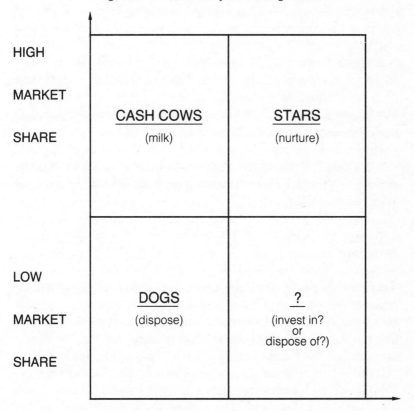

LOW MARKET GROWTH   HIGH MARKET GROWTH

share, but in a static or declining market, will be a **cash cow** to be milked in order to fund the development of new stars. Conversely, a product with only a small market share is either a **dog** if it sells to a declining market, to be disposed of at minimal cost before it absorbs too much management time and attention, or a **question mark** if the market shows attractive potential for growth. The question is whether to invest and support this product so as to build market share, or whether more attractive opportunities will exist elsewhere.

Product strengths can also be plotted by measuring other parameters, such as profitability against volume. This might lead you into niche marketing, for example, where you aim for small, specialised markets with rich profit potential because of limited competition. Alternatively, product portfolios can also be measured on a broader basis, by plotting the company's overall *business strength* (such as relative market share and product performance, price competitiveness and quality of sales support, technical back-up and geographic location) against global *market attraction* (indicated by market size and growth, price sensitivity and competition, technical sophistication, seasonality, barriers to entry, etc).

However a company chooses to plot its product strengths and weaknesses, it is important that the sales team should also understand the strategy. The communication of this should, of course, be your responsibility.

Branding

This is one of the triumphs of marketing. Even the most mundane product can be strengthened by giving it a distinctive image that reinforces the product's benefits in the customer's mind. Large, fast-moving consumer-goods companies often do this spectacularly well, heavily supported by huge promotional spends, but there is no reason why companies in other business sectors should not use similar techniques, adapted as necessary to meet local market conditions. Depending on the business sector, research shows that brand image *can* carry up to 60 per cent of the decision-making influence, while the customer's own knowledge and the supplier's/retailer's reputation carry only 30 per cent and 10 per cent respectively.

You need a name that has strong association with, and suggestions of, the image you want to portray. Make sure the name is pronounceable, does not mean something awful in another language, and can be registered with or without a selected trade mark. This brand name and its associated image should then be strongly reinforced by all your literature, packaging, advertising and other promotional support.

Product differentiation

The aim of many marketing initiatives, including branding, is to differentiate one's own product from all others in the market-place. This is especially important in the case of commodity goods, where the essential characteristics of similar products will, by definition, be the same. Unless some differentiating feature can be created, such as brand image, back-up support or special distribution arrangements, for example, many buyers will then make their purchase decisions on the basis of price, and price alone. Most companies will therefore seek to differentiate themselves from their competitors – whether in a commodity market or not – with the sole exception perhaps of those who purposely choose to ride on the back of a competitor with a 'me too' strategy.

Just how you decide to differentiate your product or service will of course depend on the specific detail that applies to your particular circumstances. However, in seeking product differentiation, be careful not to allow too many variants on the same theme to proliferate.

It may, for example, appear to be attractive to focus slightly different product variations on each of the different market segments which you have decided to attack. (We look at market segmentation in the next section.) If you take this option, be careful that the additional costs in supporting a multiplicity of brands, together with the associated problems of manufacturing and then stocking a host of product varieties, do not outweigh the benefits in the market-place.

17 Position

'I know who I am . . .'

Miguel de Cervantes

The position a product occupies in a market-place will depend upon many things, such as the way it is branded and promoted, its performance against competitors, the price and the way it is sold. The concept of position is a vital starting-point for any marketing plan: where do we *want* our product to be positioned?

There is nothing wrong with catering for the bottom end of a market, if that is what we aim to set out to capture, but clearly the sales and marketing approach will then be quite different from the one we might have adopted if we had chosen to supply the top end of the market. What happens all too often, however, is that many companies give no thought to the position they seek – until after it is too late. It is clearly much better to set out with a clear market goal from the start; then you can ensure that everything you do towards promoting and selling your product is compatible with your overall market objectives.

Segmentation

Market segmentation, as a strategic tool, focuses on how customer groups can be distinguished, rather than the *product* opportunities which we have described in the preceding section. It is a powerful marketing concept to help you decide where you want to position your product in the market and, accordingly, how your overall strategy might be targeted and structured.

The skill of market segmentation is to select the essential characteristics that identify the subsections of the market you want to participate in. These identifying characteristics could be geographic location, end-user type or size, usage rate, status, sophistication, price sensitivity, technical awareness, demand for product complexity or performance, and so on. They should be significant enough to identify the separate categories of the market which could be accessible to you, and quantifiable.

Having identified the appropriate means of dividing the market into segments, determine each segment's size by volume and value, and plot the position of each supplier. The task then is to spot the opportunities where existing suppliers are not meeting market demands, and the threats where the market may already be overcrowded.

As an example, let us suppose you are selling a new inverted reciprocating widget, and that you decide to segment the market by price sensitivity against product complexity, as in Figure 25. You have chosen these parameters because your research shows that some of your customers need very simple foolproof products, while others need much more complicated devices where price appears to be no object.

Having set up your graph, you find that the largest part of the market is indeed for relatively simple devices, which sell very cheaply. The problem is that when you come to plot your competitors' positions, they are nearly all fighting in this market area too. Your strategic choice could be to join them with a product that is even cheaper, made possible perhaps because of some technical development you have just made.

But look, the market for a more complex device is only being supplied by one company. Your market intelligence tells you that the market is small only because few of the other possible players in your market have your company's technical capabilities. As a result, this particular segment has remained underdeveloped, Better still, it turns out that the one supplier in this more complex

Figure 25: Market Segmentation – The Inverted Reciprocating Widget Market

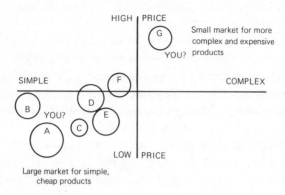

NOTE:

    Companies A to F occupy the major market for simple cheap products.
    Company G is in a totally different market segment which is small, but
    apparently underdeveloped.

STRATEGIC OPTIONS:

    · Go for a cheaper, simpler segment and sell the extra simplicity,
      perhaps with a small price advantage, or

    · Aim for a superior, more complex product than company G,
      but develop this market more aggressively, or

    · Buy company A or B.

market has his principal interests in quite different markets. This segment appears only to be a hobby to him. Clearly, you have spotted a very interesting market opportunity.

You can use this tool to identify acquisition targets too. Referring back to the example in Figure 25, if you should decide in the end to attack the cheaper, simpler market, what about buying company A or B?

Market share

Market share is a function of three subsidiary considerations:

- **Product coverage**; or that part of the total market for which you have a relevant product and which you are qualified to supply.

162

- **Market exposure**; or the extent to which your products are known to the given market and are therefore open for consideration.

- **Strike rate**; or the conversion of these enquiries to orders.

The first consideration, product coverage, is of course a matter of your **product strategy**; market exposure is a function of your **promotional activities, sales** and **distribution coverage**; while your strike rate will depend upon your **sales skills, product benefits** and **pricing strategy**. All these topics are considered in this section on marketing.

You can see therefore how important market share is as a measure of a company's overall success. It not only constitutes a measure of your overall sales and marketing ability, it also helps to pinpoint areas where you might take remedial action. As for being a barometer of competitor activity, indicating who is winning or losing in the market-place, it has no equal.

Smaller companies tend to ignore the importance of monitoring market share. For them, the difference between fourth or fifth place, for example, may seem a little academic. However, you can bet your bottom dollar that the giants in the market will be highly sensitive to their share. Smaller companies might like to reflect that one way for a larger company to establish market dominance or leadership is to buy one of the smaller players – and possibly even you!

Further, as a thought for those who are less interested in market-share league tables, it is worth reflecting on the fact that each percentage share gained is someone else's loss. In very competitive markets, where possibly too many suppliers are chasing too little business, this can be a very significant consideration.

Market leadership is not of itself an automatically good position to be in, by the way. Leadership in a market brings many advantages, but also some problems. Not the least of these is that it is often harder to defend existing market share than it is for smaller fry to nibble away at the edges of the larger company's 'bread and butter'. It only takes a little complacency by the giant for the smaller companies to have a feast at the giant's expense. If your company is a market leader, be warned – and be vigilant.

18 Pricing

'A cynic: one who knows the price of everything and the value of nothing'
Oscar Wilde

Buyers may often appear to their suppliers to be 'cynics', as described above, seeming always to emphasise their need for low prices rather than good value. In reality, however, with eyes fixed firmly on long-term profitability, many businesses will actually see their challenge today as shifting the buying emphasis more towards quality and service, rather than relying on price alone. Nevertheless, there are few markets which are not still price-sensitive, at least to some extent, even if the buying emphasis is changing. Accordingly, pricing strategy is still a most challenging and sophisticated task for any manager to have responsibility for – or, at least, it should be! As you will almost certainly have a large part to play in formulating your company's pricing strategy, you may well feel it is better to come to grips *now* with some of the options open to you, rather than later.

Cost-plus

Despite a large number of pricing tools available, it is sad to observe how many markets have been spoiled by a cost-plus strategy. Rather than charge what the market will stand, too many companies take the easy way out: they calculate the cost of their product or service and simply add a predetermined margin. This may be fine for fruit and vegetable stalls in the market-place, but not for complex businesses where, sad to relate, many don't even know accurately what their true costs are. If you suffer such unsophisticated competition, your only choice is to differentiate your product as much as you can from all the others. Then adopt an approach that allows you – and not your customers – to keep more of your precious margin.

New-product pricing

What other options to cost-plus pricing are there? For new products there are essentially two choices to make from the start:

Market penetration, where you price low to get maximum share as soon as possible. This assumes a price-sensitive market, which will not always apply, and it carries one grave disadvantage. It is always difficult to raise a price. It is much easier to lower a price later, if you need to.

The alternative choice may therefore be to go for:

Market skimming, where you content yourself with the less pricesensitive, premium end of the market first. Consideration of a price reduction can always be made later, if you should then wish to seek a larger market share.

In deciding which of these strategies to adopt, it is necessary to consider:

- **The price-elasticity of the market.** *Does* a lower price imply better market share?

- **The product's anticipated life-cycle.** There is little point in going for a market-skimming exercise if the product will have been superseded by others before you ever get your return on the development costs!

- **The size of the market, the return you can expect on your**

investment, and of course your financial resources. If your financial resources are stretched, you will probably need to maximise your return as soon as possible, even if potential longer-term gains are then prejudiced.

Other pricing strategies with which you should be familiar are:

Introductory offers. These can be used to enhance initial market penetration and customer acceptance. They need careful handling. Make it quite clear for how long you are prepared to make your special offer, or it may be an albatross round your neck for long after the product is fully launched.

Product-line enhancement. By selling at a low margin (or even a loss), the aim is to bring in sales of *other*, related products, such as spare parts or ancillary components which carry much higher margins. Once the sale of the primary product is made, sales of related products are then assured.

Diversionary pricing. This is rather similar to product-line enhancement, but this time you sell at a low price, not to promote this product, but rather to sell other products in your range which are accordingly made to look more valuable.

Predatory pricing. Such a tactic involves setting a very low price in order to kill off a competitor quickly. Be careful, however. In many markets, this can be illegal if it can be shown that you are distorting competition, or even dumping.

Price-lining. This involves setting prices in line with what your customers can afford. It is particularly favoured by those who supply tough and aggressive buyers who insist on having price reductions. The more they knock you down in price, the less they receive.

Performance-related. It can often be difficult to obtain a price premium for what you consider to be a superior product, especially if that superiority is not proven. Accordingly, the price can be made a variable, dependent upon the performance obtained in practice. The better your product works, the longer it lasts, or the more throughput your product helps to make, the more you charge.

Volume-related. This is another variable-price strategy, where the price you charge depends upon the volume purchased. This can either be through a bulk discount applied 'up-front' on the face of the invoice, or a volume-related rebate offered retrospectively over an agreed period.

Discreet pricing. In industrial markets in particular, buyers may be limited in purchasing authority. Above certain sums, they may have to seek approval from a more senior colleague or even the main board. Accordingly, the product is priced just below the discretionary purchase authority of your contact, to prevent the buying decision being referred upwards, and possibly out of sight.

Costing

In looking at pricing, it is difficult to ignore the thorny topic of costing. This should not really be a topic to be covered by a book like this, but it is vital for you to be aware of some of the key points.

First, in any complex business, the concept of a 'full cost' can be a very arbitrary calculation when it comes to allocating the company's general overheads. You may need to be prepared to engage in quite detailed discussion with your accountants about this. For example, to remove the sensitivity of volume on overhead-recovery, when costing a new product, it may be more relevant to consider 'marginal costs' only, such as labour and raw materials, and exclude all but a small proportion of the overheads of general management, administration and selling expenses. Otherwise, some new projects may never reach their true sales potential because they will be overburdened with general overheads, which the small initial volumes involved initially will be unable to support.

On the other hand, *all* costs associated with a business do need to be recovered somehow. It is very easy, for example, to forget the cost of large contingency stocks, an extended distribution channel, additional trade discounts, extended credit or special promotional activities, some or all of which may be associated with a particular product or market. It is far better to have an accurate view of a product's profit performance than to fool yourself that these 'hidden' costs do not need to be identified and recovered.

Accordingly, make a special ally of your accounts department and help them to appreciate the full commercial picture. They, in turn, can then help you understand the full financial implications of the commercial plans you have in mind.

Margin erosion

Finally, in the context of pricing, make sure that you and your team are fully aware of the effect discounts can have on profits.

First, whenever you talk about a profit margin as a percentage, be sure that everyone calculates this margin as a percentage of the *sales* value, not the cost. Many companies (and industries) talk about 'mark-up', which is based on the percentage of cost price. Look at the difference:

$$\text{MARK UP} = \frac{\text{Sales Price} - \text{Cost Price}}{\text{Cost Price}}$$

Thus a trader may buy a product at a given price and then resell it with, say 100 per cent mark-up on the cost price. This is a most illusory way of representing the true margin which, as a percentage of the sales price, is only 50 per cent:

$$\text{MARGIN} = \frac{\text{Sales Price} - \text{Cost Price}}{\text{Sales Price}}$$

The importance of all of this is that discounts are of course applied as percentages of the sales price. Thus, if you should foolishly apply a mark-up of 100 per cent, as in our example, and then offer a 50 per cent resale discount, you will mislead yourself into thinking you have kept half the profit for yourself (100 per cent minus 50 per cent). In fact, you have given all your margin away.

One of the reasons for the prevalence of mark-up as a pricing tool is that, before the era of pocket calculators, the sums were easier to do. This excuse can no longer be allowed. If you do not know how to apply a predetermined margin to a cost price, use these four simple steps which are *not* as complicated as they seem:

1) Decide the margin you want; say 30 per cent

2) Take this percentage number and subtract it from 100. Thus, in our example, $100 - 30 = 70$.

3) Now divide this number by 100 to turn it into a decimal. i.e. $\frac{70}{100} = 0.70$.

4) Take your cost price, and divide it by this decimal number. This is the sales price you now need to charge to make your requisite margin. Thus, if the cost price was £100, your sales price is $\frac{£100}{0.70} = £142.86$ (not £130!)

With practice, you will do this automatically, taking short cuts as you go. Do you want a 40 per cent margin? Then divide by 0.60 ($1 - 0.40 = 0.60$). For a 27.5 per cent margin, divide your cost price by 0.725 ($1 - 0.275 = 0.725$). Easy, isn't it?

Useful Exercise: Margin calculation

If you think all the above is hard work for little benefit, look at this example:

Fred is your sharpest salesman in the car trade. As his manager, you buy a nice little runner for £2,000 and tell Fred that the least he can sell it for is with a 25 per cent margin.

Being lazy, he applies a 25 per cent *mark-up*. The sales price is therefore £2,000 × 1.25 = £2,500. A nice little profit (note the use of the word 'little') of £500.

Now look at what this has cost you.

A 25 per cent *margin* means dividing the cost price by 0.75 per cent. This would have given a sales price of $\dfrac{£2,000}{0.75}$ = 2,666.70. Fred has just given away £166.70 – several days' wages.

Now we are all agreed on how to calculate margins, you need to indoctrinate your sales teams on the cost of discounts. In the above example, what if Fred had proposed to give away just a modest 10 per cent discount, in order to clinch the deal?

10 per cent may seem small to Fred: after all 25 per cent − 10 per cent still leaves you with 15 per cent margin. Not bad, eh, guv? But 10 per cent discount represents 40 per cent of all your total profit potential $\left(\dfrac{10 \text{ per cent}}{25 \text{ per cent}} = 40 \text{ per cent}\right)$, and he wants to give it away! Put that way, even Fred might not think the deal is quite so attractive.

19   Placement/Distribution

'There are more ways to the wood than one.'

Proverb

This topic will be of prime interest to a sales manager because its first aspect relates to how the product is to be sold. We looked at some of the considerations under **Sales channels** earlier. There may be better choices than just using an expensive field-sales force and they could include any or all of:

telephone sales,

direct mail,

agents,

distributors,

franchises.

Telesales

Telephone selling offers a very attractive low-cost option, especially for selling repeat goods of limited complexity. Whether an in-house activity or contracted out to a specialist telesales company, the key is a sound briefing and a close interface with your own order-processing and despatch function.

An in-house function can also be used for market research, sales-visit planning, sales-lead qualification and after-sales follow-up, but such an activity needs very specialised management skills to maintain enthusiasm and effectiveness.

'Telephone selling offers a very attractive low-cost option.'

Direct mail

We looked at direct mail under 'Promotion', but this powerful tool can also be used for direct *selling* into many markets. This clearly offers a low-cost opportunity, but it also demands very special skills to ensure a reasonable return. Presentation may often be the key to success, but it does not always need to be a glamorous production to catch your prospects' notice. A simple but well-presented stock-list may be just as effective as a multi-coloured glossy number, especially in industrial markets.

Agents

An agent is someone who negotiates sales on behalf of one or more principals, but is paid on commission. The contract of sale is taken by the principal. This approach offers a low-overhead entry to a market-place but, by virtue of their independence from their principals, agents may well be more difficult to manage and control.

Distributors

Distributors are also separate, independent companies, but unlike agents actually take ownership of their principals' products and then resell to the market-place. As such, the principal will usually require some minimum stocking arrangement, especially if any degree of exclusivity is to be offered.

Direct or indirect?

Figure 26 provides a summary of the comparative benefits of selling through one's own field-sales force, against selling through an agent or distributor. Note that in many export markets, and especially in countries such as the USA where sales territories can

be vast, there may be no realistic alternative to using agents, manufacturing reps and distributors, at least to start with.

Figure 26: Own Sales Team versus Distributors/Agents

1. POINTS IN FAVOUR OF HAVING ONE'S OWN SALES FORCE

ASPECT	OWN SALES FORCE	AGENTS AND DISTRIBUTORS
CONTROL	Close control/feedback	Arm's-length control
DIRECTION	Can fine-tune	Hard to focus
PRINCIPALS	One (you)	Several or many
GOALS	Yours	Theirs
TERRITORY	Relatively flexible	Relatively inflexible
OTHER DUTIES	Can be made available for other tasks	Not normally available
FUTURE GROWTH	Provides line of management succession	Expensive to replace, and no line of succession
PRODUCT KNOWLEDGE	Detailed	Restricted
COMPANY KNOWLEDGE	Know factory capabilities and people	Often, limited awareness
COMMITMENT	Long term, company-driven	Flexible commitment, market-driven

2. POINTS IN FAVOUR OF AGENTS AND DISTRIBUTORS

ASPECT	OWN SALES FORCE	AGENTS AND DISTRIBUTORS
COST	High overheads	Payment by results, BUT results by payment!
MANAGEMENT	Time-consuming	Manages self, day to day
TEST MARKETS	High risk to set up new organisation	Inexpensive, for new projects

174

3. NEUTRAL POINTS

ASPECT	OWN SALES FORCE	AGENTS AND DISTRIBUTORS
MARKET KNOWLEDGE	Specialised knowledge	Broad knowledge, based on other principals' products
USE	Richer territories	Leaner territories

One way of getting your product or service to the customer is the use of franchises, where a licence to handle your product on your behalf is granted for a specific territory, on an independent basis but under your name. Other placement options can include the setting-up of your own service or distribution depots, to cover the market on a regional basis, or even using other companies' facilities on a sub-contract basis. This latter is particularly common in the USA. If you have never given thought to alternatives such as these, they may well repay some consideration.

Transport

An area worthy of your immediate concern, under the general heading of placement, might also be transport costs and methods. This is a highly competitive arena and there are frequently attractive savings to be won by shopping around, whether or not you wish to pass these savings on to the customer.

20 Packaging

'It is only shallow people who do not judge by appearances.'
Oscar Wilde

This is another area which is often ignored by sales managers. The temptation for many, especially outside the consumer-goods industries, is to concentrate on the product and its performance, rather than the full package on offer. Packaging is often a field where it pays to employ specialist advice.

Physical protection

The most obvious requirement of any packaging should be the physical protection of the product in storage and transit, and also in use. Full consideration must be given to the rigours of the environment your product is likely to experience in each market, at home and abroad. In many applications, detailed standards of packaging may be applied by the customer, which require just as much attention as the standards applying to your product.

Visual appeal

Professional and well-presented packaging can provide a major competitive advantage, by strengthening your customers' perception of the product quality and performance. It can be especially important when used to reinforce a brand or corporate image.

Labelling

Labels are also part of packaging, and may need to carry statutory information. Nevertheless, they are an obvious part of the overall visual appeal of your products' packaging and should not be ignored.

Overall concept

Packaging, as part of the marketing mix, can also offer an important and broader concept of just what it is that you are offering your market. This concept involves recognising that you can offer your market-place much more than just a particular service or product, in terms of both real and perceived benefits. The full package that you might offer can include such traditional considerations as guarantees, special hire arrangements, tailored payment terms, extra-quick delivery and so on. But there is room for much greater imaginative effort.

When considering your product or service as a total package, what about including spare parts, any relevant and specialist tools, and so on? Some clever equipment companies even include a tin of paint for minor touch-up jobs for their plant after it has been put into service; a low-cost benefit that can be particularly appreciated by customers, indicating as it does care and attention to detail – something that can very positively reinforce a company's image in the market-place.

21 Exporting

'Travel makes a wise man better, but a fool worse.'

Thomas Fuller

All of the above considerations apply to marketing (and selling) abroad. The only real difference between selling to home markets and overseas is that distance and cultural differences (not the least of which is language) make the task of exporting vastly more difficult; but the disciplines should still be the same.

With the advent of a single European market, many would rightly argue that other European markets should be treated as extensions to the domestic UK market. However, the problems of exporting, in terms of distance and culture, remain and should not be overlooked.

Of course, contrary to the implications of the declaration made some time ago by the British government that 'Exporting is fun!', there are some very real problems to overcome. These may well include greater distribution costs and thus lower margins, special technical specifications to be met and foreign-exchange problems to be resolved.

However, in spite of these problems, companies which resolutely fail to take advantage of export markets subject themselves to two important penalties:

● they confine themselves to growth from only a small part of the global market, with all the attendant restrictions of size and opportunity, which become especially relevant when the home economy is depressed, and

- they run the risk of underestimating overseas competitors, many of whom will have ambitions in your home market too. If you do not participate in overseas markets, it is very easy to misjudge the real threat some foreign suppliers may pose back home.

Accordingly, all but small regional companies will ignore overseas markets at their peril, but that does not mean that all markets should be attacked at once. It is far better to select one or two markets and concentrate on these first, before expanding elsewhere, rather than to try and respond to all interesting possibilities at once in an unplanned and uncoordinated fashion. You wouldn't do this in your domestic market; why do so overseas?

The specific skills of exporting fall outside the scope of this book, but there are many other books on the subject to turn to, as well as assistance from other sources such as chambers of commerce, banks and even your country's embassy in the country of interest.

IV
PROBLEMS

'When are men most useless, would you say?
'When they can't command and can't obey.'

J. W. von Goethe

22 People Problems

Sales management, selling, and indeed almost all other forms of management, require strong interpersonal skills, which is why this topic was introduced early on in the Introduction. Let us now consider some of the 'problem people' you may encounter as a sales manager. They could be colleagues in your team, or elsewhere in the organisation. You may recognise some of them.

Arrogant Anthony

Tony may know more about his products and markets than anyone else in the company. Unfortunately, not only is he good, but he knows it *and* he wants everyone else to know it. He demonstrates all the qualities of a prima donna. If this is only a problem inside the company, shield him from colleagues who find him threatening or otherwise objectionable, and let him prove his prowess in the field.

If his arrogance extends to his prospects and customers, however, you have a major problem which needs to be addressed quickly before it becomes too painful for his market contacts, and your sales statistics. A lack of empathy is a major failing that probably has no redemption, and should have been spotted at the recruitment interview. Younger members of staff may well benefit from counselling and accompanied visits. Arrogance is often born out of deep-seated insecurity and immaturity; you may just possibly be able to help before it is too late. With older members of the team, however, you may find that their well-worn behaviour

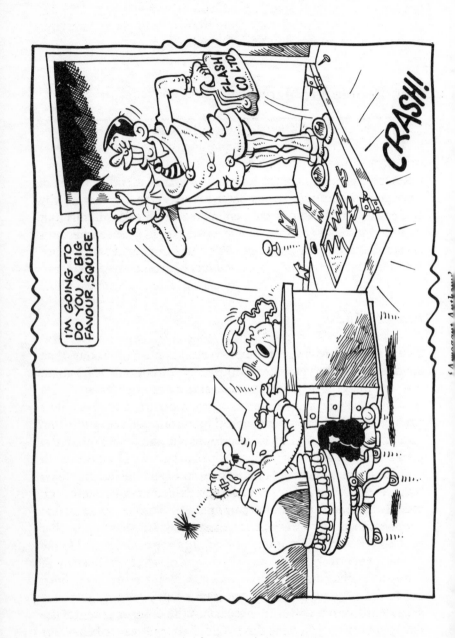

patterns cannot be changed. If so, you may well have to exercise the company's disciplinary procedures, and even consider dismissal if improvements are not made quickly.

Sensitive Sarah

Sarah is the opposite of Tony. She may have all his knowledge, but lacks the confidence. Sales people are the first to receive the brickbats from any unhappy customers, many of whom will sometimes be imagining complaints just to wring extra concessions from representatives such as Sarah. Not everyone will have the resilience to deal with such customers. Sarah and her sort can become invaluable members of a team, but they need your full-hearted support. Her problem is a serious lack of confidence in her own abilities. To help her gain confidence, consider sending her to a sympathetic customer with a genuine problem which you know she can solve, and then praise her lavishly on her successful return.

Sometimes, you may find that colleagues back at base will accuse a less aggressive representative of appearing to be far more concerned about the customers' needs than the employer's. (She just can't say no.) This requires sensitive handling by a sales manager because the perception may be quite false. We have already noted that departmental targets can conflict within the best-run companies. The only solution is to build a close liaison between them. However, the sales person who is just *too* keen to please customers, at any price, can be an expensive liability. The best solution then is to apply very tight guidelines to the authority and discretionary powers of such people, so that unacceptable concessions cannot be offered in the first place.

Naughty Nigel

Nigel's problem is one of immaturity. Away from your eagle eye, he cannot resist the temptation to fiddle his expense claims or visit reports. Perhaps he cannot say no to the drink-too-many in the pub at lunchtime, or even the shady deal which he thinks will make him a quick buck.

It is partly for such occasions that you have implemented your reporting systems, and you need to step in promptly when you suspect any such abuse. Give Nigel every opportunity to explain himself, but be ready to apply a very tight control on his future activities with the threat of dismissal for any repetition. If the offence is serious enough, you may even have to consider immediate dismissal, but be sure of your facts before acting precipitately. If an offence is proven, leniency is always inappropriate. If Nigel thinks he can get away with any breach of discipline this time, you can be certain he will be tempted to do it again, and so may others.

Moaning Minnie and Moody Max

The Minnies and Maxs of this world are an insidious problem. They may well perform quite adequately, but they spend their time with colleagues (and even worse, with customers) running down the company or its management, complaining about their bonus scheme, their back-up support, or whatever. Every instruction they are given is met with a complaint or a baleful glare and every piece of news is turned to present the worst possible interpretation. Naturally, this is highly demotivating for everyone around them.

Many people who go in for such misery-making find this is their spur, but it is at your expense and you must stop it before it poisons everyone else's attitude too. If they won't change, they must be encouraged to find employment elsewhere.

Plodding Peter

Peter, like Minnie or Max, may well meet all his targets but he appears to have little spark or enthusiasm. He is accused by the rest of his team of not giving the job his fullest efforts or attention. This response is not unnatural from a highly motivated team, but if he *is* meeting his targets you don't really have any grounds for complaint. On the other hand, you do have to consider the effect he may well have on his colleagues.

Plodding Peters can in fact be valuable members of your sales force, and they cannot all be expected to give 110 per cent of their effort, however much you may wish them to. Indeed, many Plodding Peters will show more thoroughness in dealing with their tasks than the younger tigers on your team, even if they do take longer than you would wish to do what is necessary. Make sure therefore that the plodding nature of Peter does not influence the payment of bonuses or commissions to the rest of the team, and consider reorganising his job to make the fullest use of his special talents.

Unfortunate Unwin

Sometimes a member of your staff will encounter personal adversity that is seemingly none of your business as such, but affects his or her performance. It could be marital or health problems, it might be problems with the children or other members of the family. The role of a manager must be to listen carefully and sympathetically without passing personal judgements. Someone unhappy at home will bring that unhappiness to work, just as the converse is true. A solution must be found, and your support and assistance can only help in providing that solution. Without your understanding and help, a simple problem will remain concealed and may become a major concern in due course.

There may be occasions when the problems are financial, and it is especially important to be aware of the potential knock-on effect this can cause at work, whether it is the fiddling of expenses to make ends meet, moonlighting, or any other dishonesty. If your company can help financially, it should, but only after you have found the cause of the difficulty. Involvement this way might compound the problem, so you will need to exercise great caution.

Warring Willy

Sometimes personality clashes and other such local difficulties will come to your attention. These will almost certainly require your involvement. Neither of the warring participants needs to be in the wrong for mayhem and confusion to arise. The easiest solution is to remove one or more of the parties from the others' sphere of activity. In the case of broken office romances (and even those that flourish), this may be mandatory. (See later in the next section, under *Liaisons*).

Mature adults should be able to avoid the many misunderstandings that can so easily arise and create conflict in a busy office under pressure, but, as you will know, reconciliation often requires the help of a neutral party to seal a lasting peace. This will almost certainly be your job.

Poacher Pat

Pat just hates to see a sale lost and will do anything to rescue it – no matter whose territory it is. Poaching by one sales person of another's customer is unforgivable. Your first concern must be the retention of that business, but secondly you need to address the internal problem. Read the Riot Act to Pat and consider withholding commission on the sale.

Goodbye Gordon

Gordon is going to leave you. It doesn't really matter what the reason is, his continued presence on the team is almost certainly going to be damaging. His motivation must be in question, and so must be his effect on the rest of his colleagues. Having said that, there are only very few occasions when your policy should be other than to ensure that your leaver takes with him the best possible regard for your company. Who knows what influence he may have, directly or otherwise, on future business?

188

Accordingly, remove all routine duties immediately if you can, and try to minimise the time spent clearing up or passing on special assignments. Recover all sensitive documentation, including customer records, price lists, competitor profiles and product documentation, and conduct an exit interview so that you both learn for the next time. Ensure that Gordon's company car is returned in good order, pay his salary for the remaining notice period, then wish him well and say goodbye.

This may appear to be an unattractive course of action if it leaves you understaffed. However, unless both parties are keen for Gordon to work out his full notice period, the longer-term damage that can arise from his remaining with you any longer than is absolutely necessary can often exceed the apparent short-term benefits. Further, insisting that leavers work their full period of notice can often look like what it may in fact be: spiteful.

Bully-boy Boss

You have heard that power corrupts, and absolute power corrupts absolutely. Some bosses can find that their authority over others makes them impossible to work with. If your boss is giving your staff an impossible time, you must intervene if you wish to keep your team. Tell the boss that your staff are your responsibility and that as a matter of pragmatic courtesy, communications to them should go through you. If you have a good reason for disagreeing with your boss's instructions, you have an obligation to do so. Otherwise you are as much at fault as the boss.

If working for your boss *is* impossible, then you have a simple choice. Complain to your boss's superior, unemotionally but factually, or leave. Life is too short to put up with megalomaniacs.

Finally, examine your own conscience. Is it possible that *you* may be a bully? Of course you will have to make tough demands on your team; that is part of management. But if your demands are regularly unreasonable, or unfair, or aimed only at the weaker members of your team who will not stand up to you, you have a

189

duty to change your style or look elsewhere for employment more suited to your personality.

Customer Problems

Sometimes, personal conflict will arise between a member of your team and a specific customer. Not everyone's face can fit all the time; we cannot all be compatible with everyone else.

It is folly to persist in feeding this conflict. If it is possible, try to eliminate this conflict by a change of responsibilities. On some occasions, your personal intervention with the customer may be sufficient, perhaps privately. Remember, however, that whatever solution you choose, your colleague will need to keep his or her self-esteem and confidence in order to remain an effective member of your team, just as much as will your customer.

Company Cars

The problem with company cars is not the cars, of course, but the people who drive them – and those who think they should! If your company is status-sensitive, the smallest gradation of vehicle trim or engine size will take on a significance that probably only other sales people will ever truly understand. Don't be misled by other colleagues who cannot for the life of them see the importance of a detailed car policy. Construct one, and keep to it!

23 Ethical Problems

Pressures to perform in a job can easily distort ethical judgements that might be more easily made if presented as only academic or theoretical problems. Unfortunately, we are rarely offered much guidance in the real world on how to handle the myriad ethical difficulties that can arise. In any event, they are often hard to anticipate before they are sprung upon us.

When difficult ethical judgements go wrong, they often result in considerable personal difficulty which can include loss of office and, at worst, liberty. Such problems are therefore worth considering now, in principle, before other pressures are brought to bear which may well distort your judgement of what is right, or acceptable, and what is not.

No list of potential problems can possibly be complete, nor can the answers proposed offer more than general guidance, but if this section sets you thinking about the problems, you will certainly be stronger and better prepared than if you hide your head in the sands of 'it won't happen to me'. Morality is a personal thing, but many of the following issues do stand up to a common-sense analysis which you will be well advised to consider, whatever your personal convictions.

Bribery

'I can resist everything but temptation,' said Oscar Wilde. Bribery is one temptation that should be easy for those in sales to resist, because it rarely makes sense. Consider the options. If a prospect approaches you with an order in return for some financial inducement, you may indeed gain the business. However, what will happen next time? Is it likely that you will be excused a further bribe? Of course not. Once on that treadmill, you can never get off. As the penalty for being caught in most civilised countries is gaol, is it worth it? Worse, what about your corrupt customer's colleagues? Others will be bound to find out at some stage, whether they are subordinates, superiors or at the same level. Will you be prepared to put them on the payroll too, to buy their connivance and keep their silence?

The ethical argument gets more complicated if you ask what a bribe might be. Is it a drink or a meal at lunchtime, or a bottle of whisky at Christmas? The answer to that must be a personal one, but many would say that a bribe is something offered out of the ordinary, *with the specific intention* of distorting a decision. A bottle of whisky may indeed be acceptable, but a full case? A meal may be a good way to get away from the pressures of a busy office, but can the gift of a holiday be acceptable? Probably not, you may well conclude. Equally, thanking people for an order with a small gift may be fine – but how do you feel about making the gift *before* the order is placed?

More difficult to resolve is the question of bribery overseas, where different cultures may accept (indeed, expect) rather different practices. What should your view be then? If a Third-World country is so riddled with corruption that you cannot even get your goods through customs without a bribe, what are you to do? If you accede, aren't you guilty of feeding that corruption? On the other hand, if you decline, aren't you robbing your customer of a good and otherwise honest deal – and perhaps your colleagues back home the chance of employment? If everyone else is corrupt, is it fair that *you* should suffer? You may easily decide for yourself that you could not participate in such dishonesty, but are you being fair to others in your company whose employment your scruples may well threaten, if bribery and corruption are accepted practices in that part of the world?

As an example of a real case-study, how would you have reacted to the following?

An African customer had a large order to place. The African specifying engineer contacted a potential supplier in the UK and, during the technical discussions, mentioned that his best friend, who was not as it happens even an employee of the company, had suffered a major family catastrophe. This friend's son had contracted an eye disease which would result in blindness (and indefinite unemployment) if not treated quickly. Unfortunately, no cure was available in his own country. The UK supplier's representative was asked if he could possibly arrange for the child to be flown to London for treatment, which neither the customer nor his friend's family could possibly afford.

How important was the ethical responsibility to the customer, set against the needs of a child? What would you have done?

In fact, the salesman arranged for a UK charity to see to the child's needs straight away and you will be glad to know that the operation was a complete success. You will not be surprised to learn that the UK company also picked up the business. Now, would you see this as no more than a goodwill gesture, or would you say that the particular circumstances made this humane act *de facto* corrupt in intention, if not in practice?

These are difficult questions indeed. One pragmatic solution, adopted by many companies in the West who sell regularly to countries where bribery seems to lubricate all transactions, is to appoint a local agent and pay an agreed sales commission. Then, any decision to use some of this commission for purposes that could not be condoned back home is the agent's responsibility, and his alone. You may however feel that such an arrangement is still unethical. On that, you must decide for yourself.

White lies and broken confidences

Some sales people, and many customers, believe that salesmen cannot be expected to tell the truth. As this is clearly damaging to the integrity and credibility of the sales people involved, not to mention their companies, it isn't difficult to resolve that lies will not be told. Further, lies have the obvious and practical disadvantage that they get found out, irrespective of any ethical considerations.

As with sales people, so with managers. On occasions, however, life does not permit such a simple view. Sometimes the truth can hurt more than its evasion, which may involve half-truths or white lies.

For example, you might be asked questions where the answers have to be confidential. Normally it will be sufficient to say that you are not at liberty to answer, but what about a matter of great personal importance to the questioner? Suppose you are planning some redundancies and are asked by a member of the team whether they are to be involved – perhaps before making a large investment or moving house, for example. The easiest response is to maintain confidentiality, of course. But what do you think of this?

> I was told a story, by the managing director of a company I was about to join, that he had been put in the following position some years previously. His marketing manager, who had only been with the company a few months, wanted to move house to be closer to the works. He knew that the company had been through some difficulties and was naturally keen to know how secure his job might be. He specifically asked the MD if he should delay making a move, but was given a non-committal answer. Believing that the MD would have made a signal of some sort if his job really was at risk, he moved. The manager was made redundant a week later.

Ignoring the issue of whether the post should have been filled at all in such circumstances, the MD could be said to have acted ethically in not breaking the confidence between him and his board, who were the only people to know the full situation at that time. I personally felt that the greater responsibility was to the unfortunate employee and family. You may not be surprised to learn that I did not join that company. On the other hand, however, where do you think the MD would have stood with his board if he *had* betrayed the confidence?

A similar sort of problem arises when you learn something from an employee in confidence that may have a major bearing on the firm. Maybe a colleague has divulged a serious illness to you, or that someone is about to leave, or has been up to no good. With whom do your responsibilities lie if you are specifically asked to keep the matter to yourself? Your colleague who told you or your company? You may argue that if the matter was confidential and sensitive, you should never have been told. Nevertheless, having been put in a difficult position, how do you feel about the trust that has been placed in you to keep the matter quiet? While this is still a theoretical question, you may think it a good idea to clarify your position now, before the problem should ever become a real one which may one day face you.

Dismissal

Those who have had to manage through the late seventies and the eighties may well be so accustomed to implementing wholesale redundancy that it no longer raises for them any serious ethical questions. But what responsibilities are there for a manager towards a work-force or sales team? Are there any?

At the very least, you may think that there is a serious duty of care towards individuals who are threatened with redundancy or dismissal, to ensure that these are indeed the only realistic options open to the manager concerned. You may also believe that the employer has a duty to offer every assistance in finding alternative employment. Beyond that, however, you will probably feel that the healthy survival of the company is your paramount responsibility and that your first concern must be the greatest good of the maximum number of people.

If you believe that a dismissal is really necessary, don't shirk the issue. My experience is that it is rare for such occasions to come as a complete surprise to the unfortunate individual concerned; the greatest worry is usually the uncertainty beforehand. Handle the matter sympathetically, therefore, but also straightforwardly, with confidence. Spell out the key issues clearly but briefly, and don't beat about the bush. If bad news has to be delivered, most

'I'm not going to get a gold watch, then?'

people prefer to have it early, ungarnished and without pre-varication. Don't give false hopes of reprieve if none exist. The greater part of the conversation that follows will almost invariably be about what happens next, rather than 'Why me?', which will usually only arise afterwards when the full impact of the news has sunk in.

Liaisons

We live in a society where most would believe that the private lives of employees are no one else's business. But what if that private life should spill over into the company, perhaps through an extra-marital adventure between two employees for example? Some may feel that there is a social duty to tell the injured spouse, but many others may feel that the hurt this would cause is as indefensible as the original infidelity. However, what should you do if the liaison becomes an interference with the smooth running of the company? As a manager, you may well think this is another case where you have a greater duty to the company than the individual. If it helps you to make up your mind, you may be interested to know that some American companies make it a strict personnel policy to sack immediately one of the transgressors in such circumstances, and often the more senior. In reality, one suspects that in dismissing one of the parties, the company may well end up by losing both, whether intentionally or otherwise. Nevertheless, if such a policy is well understood on joining the company, it may at least be seen to be fair, even if rather harsh.

Illegal acts

Some may, on occasion, find themselves caught in a web of intrigue that is illegal, either directly or by mere association. Apart from bribery, such intrigue could be industrial espionage (which, if it does not involve trespass, may be legal in fact, but still unethical you may think), price-fixing, tax-fiddling or whatever.

When offered a chance at the beginning not to get involved, a decision to stay uninvolved may be easy. Unfortunately, entanglement can often be insidiously progressive. You may also find pressures from your colleagues to join in or turn a blind eye, which may be difficult to resist however much you may want to.

If you ever find yourself in such a position, you may then find it is too late to withdraw. Clearly the fact that others are engaged in illegal activity – however widespread – cannot excuse you. This is why it is important for you to take a view of such matters *before* you ever become involved.

In fact, life is never simple. Some activities which are clearly illegal may not in fact offend your code of ethics. What do you do then? The easiest and wisest counsel is to obey the law in any event, but you will know that the law is not always very consistent. For example, there are strong rules on what you can do commercially in European markets, but those same rules do not always apply to you as a European operating *outside* those markets. Accordingly, whether or not it is ethically right, it may be quite permissible for you to carve up markets, organise cartels and restrict competition overseas, as long as you don't engage in such practices inside Europe.

More than this, if an act is not illegal, so that others can and do engage in such practices, you may also be obliged to follow suit or suffer the commercial consequences, whatever your ethical view of the matter. Perhaps the best solution is to formulate very strong views on the simple issues, be more flexible on the difficult ones, and get to know a good international lawyer!

'Obscene' profits

It may seem strange that anyone should complain about turning an honest penny, but an occasion might just perhaps arise when your conscience is pricked by an excessively large margin, perhaps resulting from very special market opportunities.

Now you may think it is rather naïve to complain about any opportunity to make a market 'killing'; isn't that what all sales people seek? You may be annoyed by the only ice-cream salesman in the park, for example, who doubles his prices on a very hot day, but no one need feel obliged to buy from him if they are offended by his opportunism.

Just occasionally, however, you may feel that there are some pricing activities which are clearly unacceptable. As an extreme, you might think of racketeers who make exorbitant profits from selling food parcels sent by charity to Third-World countries suffering from drought or famine. Clearly, anyone who benefits from such an 'opportunity', caused by others' misery or misfortune, is not commercially shrewd but actually unethical.

Other examples which are less obvious may just perhaps cross *your* path. On such occasions, you may feel it is sufficient to examine your own conscience and be guided by it. However, if you feel your ethical judgement is in doubt, be pragmatic. Consider the effect of your opportunism on your customers. If you would be offended *as a customer*, so might they. Then ask yourself: can you afford to upset your customers this way?

24 Profit – and the Lack of It

Sometimes your best-laid plans may go wrong and your profit targets badly astray. It may be that a major market which you serve suddenly collapses, or a major customer withdraws their business from you for whatever reason, or a competitor suddenly steals a large slice of your market share. At such times, extra skills and resourcefulness are required by everybody in the company. As sales manager, you have a special role to play.

Volume

Lost volume can be a dramatic event for any business. If it cannot be regained quickly, your managing director will be obliged to seek equivalent reductions in fixed overheads, and that will almost certainly mean reductions in people. Your first job, however, is to regain that volume, if at all possible.

To do that, you need not only to know what the symptoms are, but also the causes. Obviously, the earlier the diagnosis, the quicker the appropriate remedies may be applied. If you have lost a major customer, is it because he has closed down? In which case, who will have picked up his market share? Or is it because you have failed as a supplier in some way? The symptom may be the same, but the causes very different. Different causes will require quite different remedies.

If the problem is caused by a fundamental weakness in your product, this must clearly be remedied quickly – and honestly. If, alternatively, the cause is the collapse of a major customer, unless the loss of business is huge, the well-organised manager should not be too sorely troubled for long. This is when your carefully developed data base comes into its own. Trawl your prospect bank for all those potential customers whom you have never had time to explore fully and send out the storm-troops. Make it fun and run a competition for who can bring in the most new business. Review the 'top thirty customer' list and squeeze every last drop of additional market share from it that you can. If things are bad, redouble your mail shots and make your unbeatable special offers. If you haven't done so already, review every lapsed customer who has ever bought from you in the past, review all your old leads, and chase them like fury. Identify the key areas of attention and throw your full weight behind them; do not allow yourself – or your available resources – to be side-tracked.

Finally, if it does come down to reducing fixed overheads, be realistic. Do not try and defend 'your' department against others. You need to find every way possible to drive down the burden of overheads you cannot pay for, and the sooner the better.

Contingency planning

One of the best positions to be in, if you ever face such a catastrophe, is to have planned for it in advance, just in case. Disappearing markets are usually foreseeable, whether for economic, political or technological reasons. If so, you are negligent in your duties not to have planned ahead. Should your company not have such a contingency plan, don't leave it until it is too late. Sit down with your colleagues, now, and plan one.

Margins

Although a loss of volume can be more dramatic, more insidious is a loss in margin, and this is often the first place to look for lost profits. A small loss in margin can often have a far greater effect on profits than a relatively large loss in volume.

Lost margin can be due to a number of causes: for example, product-mix changes, cost increases or price discounting (see under 'Pricing').

Adverse product-mix changes can be hard to counteract, but the quickest remedy is to re-examine your pricing policy. Maybe your markets *will* stand a higher price on some of your leaner-margin items. (If they do not, you may have to consider withdrawing them – which, by the way, is an excellent method of finding out how price-sensitive these so-called 'dogs' really are. They may become 'stars' yet! We discussed this under 'Products' in the Marketing section.) Conversely, some of your richer products may be over-priced: they are just no longer competitive in the market-place. If so, you should ask yourself why your sales force hadn't alerted you much earlier!

Some cost increases can perhaps be fought off or delayed, but if this is a cause of your problems, you must consider recovering them as soon as possible. Do so, now.

If price-discounting is your problem, you have probably given your team too much leeway in their pricing responsibilities. Examine every contract you have, starting with the largest, and if necessary attempt to renegotiate them. This may sound a daunting task, but having done it myself on occasion, I can assure you it is not so impossible as you may think. If you have paid proper attention in the past to cultivating your key markets, you may find your customer base is far more loyal than you might expect. Strong customers need strong suppliers: it should not be in their best interests to lose you if you have looked after them well in the past.

Expenses

Whatever the cause of your problems, the possible remedies are unlikely to exclude an additional scrutiny of expenses, *as well*. Starting with the largest items first, look ruthlessly at every out-going expense under your control. Is it essential? Can it be postponed? Can it be reduced? Of course, when there are problems

'Don't forget that you should share in these cut-backs too.'

in the market-place, there will naturally be some reluctance to prune the sales activity and promotion budget which brings the sales in. However, special times call for special remedies. Do you really need to go to that exhibition? Can you do without that catalogue reprint for a bit longer? Do you really have to dispense all those trade gifts and hospitality?

If times are tough, consider also the psychological aspect. Have no reluctance in sharing the information, no holds barred, with all your staff. You are not seeking to panic them, but you are calling for an extra special effort. In order to reinforce this, consider asking for sacrifices, *even if they are not strictly necessary*. Cutting back on meal allowances, stopping the odd trade journal, or insisting that all telephone calls are made at the cheap rate, may not have a major effect on your profitability, but such actions do have a powerful signalling effect that the problem is real, and needs everyone's contributions and co-operation. Don't forget that you should share in these cut-backs too, and your senior colleagues.

25 Competition – and How to Respond

There is no doubt that, with the accelerated growth in communications technology and the shrinking of national frontiers, competition in nearly all markets is increasingly becoming more international – and tougher. Moves for a single European market reinforce this trend. Accordingly, the first requirement is *market intelligence*. In other words, who is doing – and going to do – what, where and how? Then you need a *strategy*, which must be flexible. The analogy of military strategy in planning a commercial defence and offence is very fitting here, which may explain why one of the most successful marketing managers in the European steel industry in recent times was trained not in marketing, but in military history!

Proactive offence

Clearly the best defence against competition is offence. This means taking action, *preferably in advance* of any actual threat, to protect market shares and profits. This is the role of product development and enhancement (see earlier under 'Product', in the Marketing section), coupled with aggressive sales and marketing development, and even acquisition. The stronger you are, the less daring competitors will be in attacking you for fear of retaliation. Equally, the more resilient and resourceful you will be in making that counter-attack. Further, the stronger your position in any given market, the weaker your competitors will be.

205

Reactive defence

Clearly, proactive offence *before* you are attacked is a vastly superior strategy to reacting afterwards. However, even the best-laid plans cannot cover the options so completely that your pro-active 'offensive defence' is entirely sufficient. Sometimes even the best-prepared companies will be taken by surprise. You will then need a reactive defence. What are your options?

Pricing

The traditional approach to an incursion by a competitor into 'your' market is to react by trimming prices. New competitors who do not have any marked product differentiation are almost obliged to adopt a low-price market-entry strategy, in order to gain access. If you respond by matching the price cuts made by your competitor, the major beneficiary will naturally be your customer, but such a response can work if your pricing signal is immediate and severe. Unfortunately, it can result in a damaging price war and whoever wins will always face the problem of trying to restore price levels later. This is never an easy prospect.

You can of course choose to do nothing and rely on market inertia. This may be the best reaction if you have well-placed confidence in the strength of your product and service but, if this confidence is misplaced, it could be a very costly mistake.

As an alternative, you may instead choose to react by attacking one of your competitor's own key markets, as a tactic to signal 'If you hurt me, I'll hurt you'. To do this well, you need to have sufficient market strength for the threat to be real and for the competitor to feel that he has at least as much to lose as he might gain. It is clearly an approach that carries some risk, but at least it serves to highlight the need to attend to basic marketing principles in building strong market positions from the outset.

Finally, you can also protect your market share on occasion by tying up your customer base with long-term contracts. This will almost invariably mean offering some price-related inducement, but it can be a powerful method over the short and medium term.

Promotion

As an alternative to responding to competition with a pricing initiative, you can look at some of the other 'Ps' which make up the marketing mix, described earlier. An increased promotional spend is one alternative, which is an option you will see used regularly by the fast-moving consumer-goods industry, for example. It is actually very difficult for new entrants to break into well-developed markets, and anything that reinforces your brand image and customers' loyalty (or inertia) must be to your additional advantage.

A problem with an increased promotional spend is that the effects can be relatively short-lived, especially if the competitor takes following action and increases his promotional activity too. It can also be very expensive. However, if your product is already heavily branded, you may be obliged to protect the brand this way in any event.

Product modification

If you are able to, consider as well – or instead – a modification to the product. A relaunch of a slightly modified product, or even a new one, is a very powerful response to unwelcome competition, although obviously limited by your resources. Unless you have such a reply already planned, however, you are unlikely to be able to respond quickly enough to prevent considerable damage to your share.

Product package modification

If some form of product development or modification is not possible, then look at all the other aspects of your overall product package, including service, guarantee, delivery, payment terms, spare parts etc. Changes to your package may indeed be hidden price reductions, but they are much easier to withdraw later.

'Knocking' copy

As a last thought on competitor activity, it is worth commenting on libel, slander and lesser forms of hurting competitors. The first rule is universal: NEVER knock your competitors. Innuendo and less subtle methods of diminishing competitors' credibility are invariably damaging in the market-place; they belittle your company's stature and they can develop into a mud-slinging battle. By all means say why your products are better, your service is slicker and your company is stronger, but don't say your competitor is failing, his products are inadequate and his service non-existent, even if it is true.

If your customer has also bought from this competitor, you are overtly criticising his judgement and acumen. If your competitor does have faults (and few will be perfect), your buyer should be alllowed to infer these from the strength of your own company's offering and salesmanship. If your allegations are false, you will lose your customers' respect and your credibility with them.

What are you to do if competitors start knocking you? Often, you will want to let them demean their own standing by what is generally seen as unprofessional conduct, and do nothing overtly, but you might still contact these competitors and insist that they stop. Very often, mud-slinging starts at quite junior levels in the sales hierarchy and it might be that the senior management is not aware of what is going on. Sometimes, however, mud thrown can stick. In such circumstances, analyse carefully what is being said and what your market-place actually believes. If there is truth in the allegations, attend to your shortcomings promptly and reinforce your strengths. If the allegations are without foundation, deny them, reinforce your PR and consider litigation.

26 Sales Meetings and Conferences

You may wonder why this topic appears under the banner of Problems. The answer is simple: sales meetings can be disastrous unless you plan them carefully and follow some basic rules.

Gathering your sales team together regularly is an important means of ensuring good and effective communications, for sharing market intelligence and new product knowledge, for building team spirit and unity of purpose. It is accordingly far better to hold sales meetings little and often, rather than rarely but spectacularly. However, the benefits of an occasional extravagance of venue and presentation should not be underestimated, especially as an aid to motivating the troops.

Whatever the style of your meetings, the golden rules include:

- **Always have a reason for meeting, and if possible a focus.** Don't meet just for the sake of it. Taking expensive sales people off the road unnecessarily is expensive. Equally, a strong and relevant theme which runs throughout the meeting is much more powerful (and memorable) in its effect than a long shopping list of unrelated points made one after the other.

- **Plan every part of your meeting down to the last detail.** Never take for granted that everything will be all right on the day: invariably it won't be. If the venue is not known to you, check it out and make personal contact with the manager. Get to know the geography of your venue, including the location of lavatories and bars, ensure that

209

your requirements for flip-charts, slide projectors and so on are fully understood, check that you will not be disturbed by neighbouring events and other distractions, and plan every moment of the day.

- **Vary the diet.** Don't make every meeting an opportunity for *you* to spend the time talking. Involve other colleagues in making presentations, engage outside speakers, vary the presentations to include not just talks but discussions, training films, a works visit, and so on, and allow for regular moments of light relief. Concentration spans vary, but do not assume that you can hold the rapt attention of any of your assembled company without breaks for recuperation.

- **Prepare and rehearse.** The art of public speaking does not come readily to many, and there is nothing worse than a well-intentioned speaker who drones on and on, however valuable the message being delivered. If your meeting has a central theme, make sure that this is fully understood by all of your contributors so that each session links with the next. Ensure also that overhead slides and other graphics are clearly produced, legible and relevant. If you plan to use other contributors, make sure that you know what equipment they will need to assist their presentations. If they are not familiar with the venue or what is expected of them, make sure that they are properly briefed in advance. This should include information on how many people they will be addressing and the size of the room. Unless there are only a few delegates, you can be sure that someone will have trouble reading overhead slides that have been reproduced from typewriter-sized print; have these produced professionally if you have any doubt.

   One more thought on planning: unless it is totally impracticable, insist that your contributors rehearse, and preferably in the room you will be using.

- **Make sure your speakers know the rules of good presentation.** Do they know to whom they will be speaking and what their audience needs to know? Do they know that a good presentation demands the three Es of Enthusiasm, Energy and Excitement? (Don't let them read from a script; ask them to speak from short notes.) Will there be a clear beginning, a middle and an end? Will they build to a climax? Remind them to make frequent pauses in their delivery, to look the audience in the eye (and *not* at a screen or flip-chart) and encourage them to ask the audience questions.

- **Appoint a knowledgeable chairperson.** Unless your gathering is very informal, your team will require signals of what is to happen, when, and whether they are to be encouraged to interrupt and ask questions (always preferable) or not. If you are not to be the chairman, which can be beneficial if your meeting needs an impartial or independent leader, ensure that he or she is at least sufficiently knowledgeable and senior to ensure that the meeting stays on course and that red herrings are avoided.

- **Try to look forwards – as well as backwards.** Reviews of past performance are important and can be highly instructive, but alone they can also become boring and introspective. When spelling out the lessons of the past, don't forget to draw out their implications for future changes in tactics or strategy, including – of course – new product or business development.

- **Review the results and incorporate lessons learned for the next time.** Unless you are an experienced hand at this sort of thing, you will be amazed at the innumerable possibilities for disaster that lurk at every turn, sometimes quite literally. I once planned a conference at a delightful country house which was only to be found by leaving a desolate by-way and turning up a long, winding drive. Only on arrival did I find that the only sign-board for the venue at the entrance to the drive had been taken down for repainting!

In fact, there was no problem. First, everyone had been

sent much more detailed travelling instructions than those provided by the venue's own staff, which alone is a useful tip. Secondly, I had been there before, so at least *I* knew where the venue was. Finally, I also had the good fortune to arrive early, another essential piece of advice. I was therefore able to post someone at the entrance to the drive, to ensure that no one following me might miss the turning. If I hadn't taken at least one of these precautions, I might have found myself organising a very interesting initiative test, but it would have been a very peculiar conference!

27 You – and Your Career

From all that has gone before, you will be in no doubt that managing your job and your team is going to exercise your talents fully. You will need to apply all your drive, enthusiasm and skill. You will need to enthuse, motivate and encourage. You will need to be imaginative, organised and entrepreneurial. Your tasks will probably occupy most if not all of your waking hours. They should also reward and fulfil you.

With such responsibilities, it would be easy to ignore your family. They need your support, as you will need theirs. But there is also someone else, very important, whom we have left out: you.

Too many excellent managers fail to attend to their own needs and, specifically, their careers. They spend every moment concerned with their team, their products and the market-place, with their colleagues and their bosses, so that it is not surprising that they spend little time attending to their own career development. Sadly, unless their management is equally excellent, their own training and development needs will tend to be forgotten. Eventually, successful and proficient though such managers may be, they will rule themselves out of the running for further promotion and others will move on instead. Not surprisingly, this can sow seeds of dissatisfaction and despair. Under such circumstances, even the best managers will eventually diminish their own worth. This can be a tragic waste of talent and commitment; don't let it happen to you.

Naturally, it is clear that some sense of selfless dedication is essential if you are going to perform well in your job. However, the manager who, at the other extreme, spends all his or her time solely concerned with his or her own career is never going to build a strong team, nor probably earn much respect from peers and bosses. Accordingly, give your fullest attention to the job in hand, but also make time to review your progress with your superiors at regular intervals. Consider what your next job might be and determine what additional skills you will need to cultivate in order to qualify for it.

Appraisals

In the same way that you need to appraise your own staff of their performance, so you need to be appraised yourself. In engaging your own boss in such a discussion, make it clear what your ambitions are. Review together your objectives, and your progress. Obviously you will want to establish how your career goals may be achieved within your present company, but do not be afraid to reconcile yourself to a view that you may have to look elsewhere for promotion, in due course.

Looking elsewhere

Should you ever get to the stage of looking elsewhere for career advancement, there are two possibilities. One choice is to seek alternative employment covertly, for fear that your present post would immediately be placed in jeopardy. This may be a frequently felt and valid concern, but there is a better option if you are fortunate. If you have tended your relationship with your immediate superior carefully and diligently, the spirit of trust and integrity that you enjoy should allow you to discuss such matters in frank confidence together. No one likes losing a good employee, but losing one unexpectedly is worse. No mature boss should therefore ignore the opportunity of first exploring responsibly, perhaps with other senior staff and colleagues, all the alternative options that may be open to you internally: which is indeed just what *you* would surely want to do if the roles were reversed.

I wish you every good fortune, success and satisfaction in growing your own career, and indeed the careers of your staff. I very much hope that you will find reading this book to have been of help to you.

Suggested Reading

Having suggested in the Introduction that it was a fallacy that sales teams and their managers are too busy to read management and business books, I don't intend that you should feel obliged to read all of the following! However, may I encourage you to read some of these, at least? Scavenge your public or company library, be proud of your own collection, and pass on the knowledge and wisdom you acquire. Here is an abbreviated list reflecting my personal choice which I have found useful, or have recommended to colleagues with positive feedback. They are listed in the same approximate order as the topics in this book.

Management

The Business of Management, R. Falk, Pelican. Although first published in 1961, still full of sound common sense with many practical examples.
Call Yourself a Manager! M. Archer, Mercury Books. Well produced, quick and light to read, and none the worse for that.
Industrial Administration and Management, J. Batty, Macdonald and Evans. The title says it all.
Handbook of Management, D. Lock and N. Farrow, Gower. A giant tome covering most aspects of business management, designed mainly as a reference book but worth more frequent dipping into than that might otherwise suggest.
Making it Happen, J. Harvey-Jones, Collins. Personal reflections

of one very successful manager, appropriately subtitled *Reflections on Leadership*.
What They Really Teach You at the Harvard Business School, F. J. and H. M. Kelly, Piatkus. Not all of it, of course, but a good flavour of what to expect if you see your career might benefit from an MBA or equivalent.

Data handling

Modern Businees Statistics, J. E. Freund and F. J. Williams, Pitman. Covers statistics for many business uses, including production.
Spreadsheet Marketing, A. West, Gower. If you do not want to buy tailored packages and already enjoy some computer literacy, this is for you. Otherwise, give it to a colleague for Christmas!

People

Understanding Organisations, C. B. Handy, Penguin. A 'must' in 1976, and it still is. Of more relevance to larger companies, it will still illuminate many a path in smaller organisations.
52 Ways to Develop Your Staff, Trish Nicholson, Mercury Books (W. H. Allen). Strong on personal development, of yourself and the team. (Heard some of this before? I hope so, or you haven't been reading this very thoroughly!)
Creating the Hands-On Manager, W. Watts, Mercury Books (W. H. Allen). Just as it says, with some interesting comments on psychological profiling and how to use it.
Conversation Control Skills for Managers, C. J. Margerison, Mercury Books (W. H. Allen). How to resolve problems and seize new opportunities with your team – and others.
Body Language, A. Pease, Sheldon Press. How to interpret what people *really* mean at work, and elsewhere.

218

Selection

Great Answers to Tough Interview Questions, M. J. Yate, Kogan Page. Not just for those on the move, but very stimulating for interviewers too.

Negotiating

Managing Negotiations, G. Kennedy, J. Benson and J. McMillan, Hutchinson. Now an award-winning Rank training film. A good introduction to what some make a life-time's work (see below).
How to Negotiate Better Deals, J. G. Thorn, Mercury Books. I'm told it is very readable. It was also meant to be very comprehensive and a useful training tool for others – still a life-time's work!
The Skills of Negotiating, W. Scott, Gower. Another good introduction, that should leave you wanting to know more.
Negotiating Behaviour, D. G. Pruitt, Academic Press. The most readable summary of the last few decades' research work in the English-speaking world that I have yet found.

Sales management

How British Industry Sells, G. Brand and F. Suntook, Industrial Market Research. Published in 1976, it is still one of the most comprehensive surveys of the UK sales management scene, which is why I have quoted liberally from it where the data uncovered still carries some relevance.
The Sales Direction Survey of Sales Management, Sales Direction Magazine Ltd and The Management Information Exchange Ltd. Published in 1989, this is a statistical *tour d'horizon* of UK sales management practice. Although it only enjoyed a limited number of respondents (174 companies, against 301 in the survey mentioned above), it covers a much broader range of businesses, including retail, fashion, fast-moving consumer goods,

publishing, transport and information technology. The approach is didactic and consciously seeks to uncover omissions, but accordingly gives much informative guidance.

Managing a Sales Force, M. T. Wilson, Gower. A slightly daunting format, but complemented by useful charts and other ideas. It is especially interesting on character traits with regard to recruitment.

The A–Z of Sales Management, J. Fenton, Pan. Written by possibly the best-known salesman in the UK, the format is selective but it makes a very enjoyable read and still sells well even though it was published in 1979.

Marketing

Marketing Management, P. Kotler, Prentice-Hall International. The Grand-daddy of them all. Unless you have no interest in strategic marketing at all, buy this – even if you never buy another book.

Marketing for the Small Business, D. Waterworth, Macmillan. A title that undersells an excellent and very practical résumé of the topic.

To Catch a Mouse, Make a Noise Like a Cheese, L. Kornfeld, Radio Shack (Tandy Corporation). Written when Mr Kornfeld was vice-president of Radio Shack, it reads like its title: zany but wonderful.

Improve your Profits . . . Satisfying Customers, R. Sewell, Mercury Books. I think I recognise the quotation – page 18 of Mr Falk's book mentioned above, and nothing wrong with that. Highly readable, well presented and great for a regular dip into.

The Winning Streak, W. Goldsmith and D. Clutterbuck, Penguin. A review of 'Britain's top companies' and the lessons they teach us. Not to be ignored.

In Search of Excellence, T. J. Peters and R. H. Waterman, Warner Books. The American forerunner of *The Winning Streak*, with similar messages.

The Decline and Rise of British Industry, D. Clutterbuck and S.

Crainer, Mercury Books. More of what we did wrong, and what we now do right. Well, most of us.

Take a Chance to be First, Warren Avis, Macmillan. Yes, Mr Avis himself, now moved on from car hire. This claims to offer 'Hands-on Advice from America's Number One Entrepreneur', with chapters like 'Why Lone Rangers Make Lousy Entrepreneurs'. (Worth noting that they also make lousy customers too, some of them.)

Industrial Marketing Digest. A quarterly magazine that teaches more per issue, for those interested specifically in industrial marketing, than any other journal around. Based mainly on practising managers' experience, it is well worth subscribing to.

Think Marketing, M. van Mesdag (Mercury Books). The importance of market orientation throughout management at all levels.

Exporting

Managing Export Marketing, B. Katz, Gower. Mainly for the newcomer, well presented and easy to read. An excellent introduction to the subject.

International Sales and the Middleman, John G. Griffin (Mercury Books). The importance of managing your agents and distributors is often overlooked.

Index